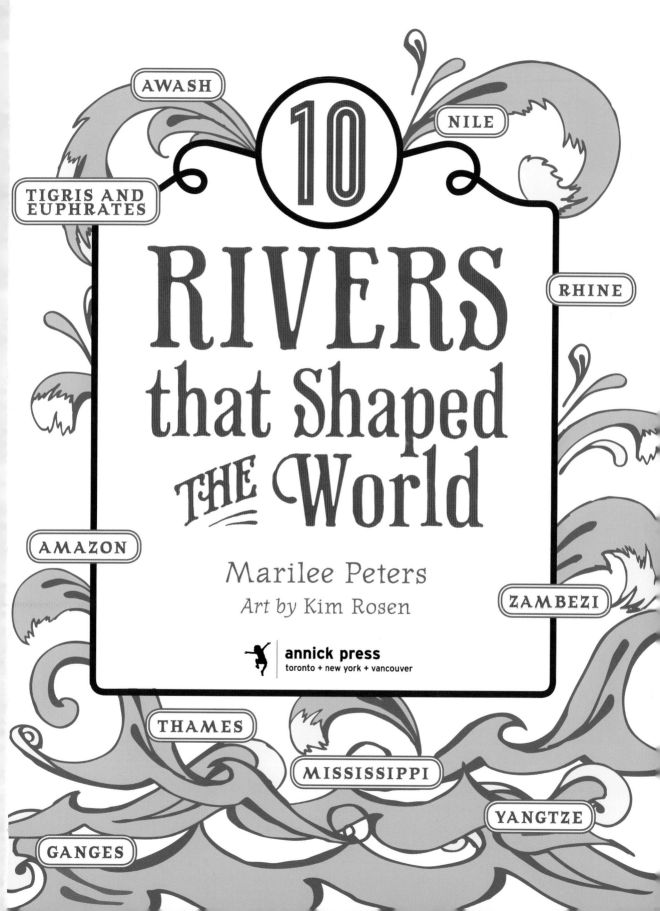

AWASH

NILE

TIGRIS AND EUPHRATES

RHINE

10
RIVERS
that Shaped
THE World

Marilee Peters

Art by Kim Rosen

AMAZON

ZAMBEZI

annick press
toronto + new york + vancouver

THAMES

MISSISSIPPI

YANGTZE

GANGES

Edited by Barbara Pulling
Proofread by Elizabeth McLean
Designed by Natalie Olsen/Kisscut Design

Annick Press Ltd.

We acknowledge the support of the Canada Council for the Arts, the Ontario Arts Council, and the Government of Canada through the Canada Book Fund (CBF) for our publishing activities.

ONTARIO ARTS COUNCIL
CONSEIL DES ARTS DE L'ONTARIO
an Ontario government agency
un organisme du gouvernement de l'Ontario

Cataloging in Publication
Peters, Marilee, 1968–, author
10 rivers that shaped the world / Marilee Peters ; art by Kim Rosen.

Includes bibliographical references and index.
Issued in print and electronic formats.
ISBN 978-1-55451-739-8 (bound).—ISBN 978-1-55451-738-1 (pbk.).—
ISBN 978-1-55451-740-4 (html).—ISBN 978-1-55451-741-1 (pdf)

1. Rivers—History—Juvenile literature. 2. Rivers—Social aspects—History—Juvenile literature. I. Rosen, Kim, 1978–, illustrator II. Title. III. Title: Ten rivers that shaped the world.

GB1203.8.P48 2015   j551.48'3   C2014-906751-8
                                              C2014-906752-6

Distributed in Canada by:
Firefly Books Ltd.
50 Staples Avenue, Unit 1
Richmond Hill, ON L4B 0A7

Published in the U.S.A. by Annick Press (U.S.) Ltd.
Distributed in the U.S.A. by:
Firefly Books (U.S.) Inc.
P.O. Box 1338
Ellicott Station
Buffalo, NY 14205

Printed in China

Visit us at: www.annickpress.com
Visit Marilee Peters at: www.marileepeters.ca
Visit Kim Rosen at: www.kimrosen.com

Also available in e-book format. Please visit www.annickpress.com/ebooks.html for more details. Or scan

CONTENTS

For Tom, whose love and support make it all possible. —M.P.
For my parents, who never discouraged me from pursuing art. —K.R.

Introduction

IMAGINE THIS: you're the leader of your country, and you're worried. You're starting to lose your influence—your grip on power is getting weaker by the day. What can you do to show people you're still a forceful leader, and inspire their trust again?

For Mao Zedong, the leader of China from 1949 until the 1970s, the answer was simple: swim across the Yangtze, the country's biggest, strongest, most famous river. So that's what he did. When he arrived dripping and breathless on the far side, the whole country considered him a hero, and Mao was able to stay in power long enough to shape the future of China.

River marshlands are home to the Ma'dān people of Iraq

Mao wasn't the only one to realize that rivers are important symbols. For hundreds of years, leaders have known that by showing they have power over rivers, they can impress people, or intimidate them, or even change history. In 55 BCE, Julius Caesar had his troops build the first bridge over the Rhine River, a feat that startled the Germanic tribes of Europe so much, they gave up on attacking Rome (for a while). And when the Tigris River wasn't a reliable enough source of water for his palace gardens, King Sennacherib of ancient Mesopotamia had miles of aqueducts built to divert its water. The result is thought to have been the fabled Hanging Gardens of Babylon—one of the wonders of the ancient world.

Then there was the shogun of Japan, who refused to allow the flood-prone Tone River to destroy his brand-new palace in the little town of Edo. He had workers dig for 50 years to create a new channel for the river, sending it a safe distance away. Today, that little town the shogun saved has become one of the world's biggest cities.

Powerful leaders like these, who command armies of workers and possess unlimited amounts of money, can sometimes manage to control rivers and change history. But more often, it's the rivers that are in charge.

For many people around the world, their way of life and even their survival depends on rivers. Take the Ma'dān people of Iraq, who live in the middle of a vast marshland where the Tigris and Euphrates rivers meet. They live on floating platforms anchored to palm trees, build their homes from reeds and clay scooped from the riverbanks, and paddle around in reed boats. They eat fish and wild birds, grow rice along the riverbanks, and keep water buffalo. The river gives the Ma'dān everything they need to survive.

You might think that's an extreme example of a river's influence, but here's another one. Hundreds of years ago, the Rhine River in Europe was edged by dozens of little kingdoms. They were always warring with each other—until they were forced to band together to drive out the robber barons who were holding up ships and making

life miserable for everyone. Today, European countries are using the lessons they've learned from centuries of cooperation along the Rhine to join forces against a new enemy: industrial polluters that are endangering the life of the river.

But what happens when the river you've come to depend on changes? After all, rivers can be fickle—sometimes they alter their course, or flood, or even dry up. Today, the Indus River in southern Pakistan trickles through a desert landscape. But thousands of years ago, cities flourished along its banks, making up a major civilization known as the Harappan Empire. Never heard of it? That's because the Indus changed its course, and seemingly overnight the Harappan civilization crumbled. That's the power of a river.

The 10 stories that you'll read in this book explore the dramatic and varied ways that rivers have shaped us, and the ways that we've tried—sometimes successfully, sometimes with unforeseen consequences—to shape them. It all begins with where we came from...

1

AWASH

A River of Bones

NAME
The Awash is also called *Wehaietu*
in the Afar language of Ethiopia.

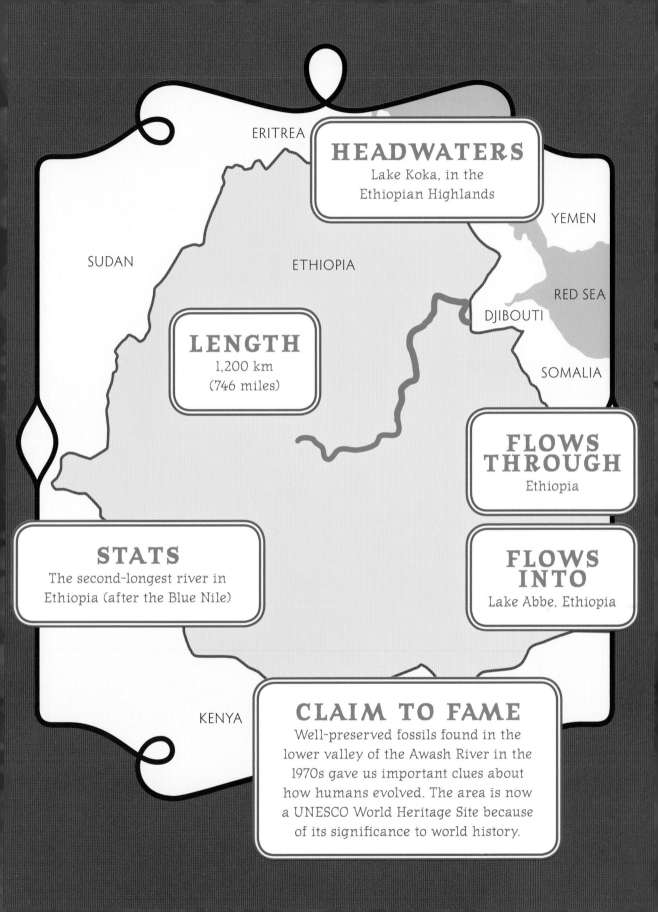

ERITREA

HEADWATERS
Lake Koka, in the
Ethiopian Highlands

YEMEN

SUDAN

ETHIOPIA

RED SEA

DJIBOUTI

SOMALIA

LENGTH
1,200 km
(746 miles)

**FLOWS
THROUGH**
Ethiopia

STATS
The second-longest river in
Ethiopia (after the Blue Nile)

**FLOWS
INTO**
Lake Abbe, Ethiopia

KENYA

CLAIM TO FAME
Well-preserved fossils found in the
lower valley of the Awash River in the
1970s gave us important clues about
how humans evolved. The area is now
a UNESCO World Heritage Site because
of its significance to world history.

ETHIOPIA
[3 MILLION YEARS AGO]

The little ape scuttled along, hoping to escape the burning orange gaze of the afternoon sun. She should have been asleep with her babies, high up in the branches of a mahogany tree amid the cooling breeze, but she'd been driven out of the shelter of the trees by one thing: hunger. Her family hadn't eaten for several days. Now she was desperate. So desperate that she'd ventured out into the savanna to seek food.

She sped through the grassy meadow. It wasn't safe here; she didn't dare stop to look for food yet. The grass was so tall she could barely see over it to watch for enemies, and it offered no cover. She needed to get to the river. She'd find shade and shelter in the bushes there, and plenty of fruit to pick from the low-hanging branches. The ape could already smell the fresh river air, and almost taste the coolness of the water. She would eat and drink her fill, then gather fruit to carry back to her babies.

At last she made it to the river. She picked her way down the steep bank to the water's edge, dipped her hands in, and scooped up dripping mouthfuls. Bliss.

But as she crouched in the shallows, the ape mother was unaware of a new danger. In the mountains far above, it had been raining torrentially for days. A hundred swollen streams had raced into the river. Now, a huge flash flood was pounding downstream. With a sudden roar, a wall of water as tall as an elephant surged around a bend and crashed into the tiny ape, tossing her up and carrying her along in a churning flow of white water.

Days later, as the water levels in the river returned to normal, the little ape mother's body came to rest on the riverbed. Layers of fine dirt and sand in the water sifted down, covering her over. Time passed, and her small bones slowly fossilized in their river grave. Waiting ...

The Story of the Awash

The Awash River is born in the rainy green hills of Ethiopia's fertile highlands. The river hurtles downhill at great speed, tumbling through steep gorges until it reaches the broad, bare plains of the Danakil Desert. Then it slows, winding its way lazily through the desert to the Afar Triangle, which at 156 meters (512 feet) below sea level is one of the lowest places on earth.

Today, the Afar Triangle is also one of the most inhospitable places on earth: a salt flat where every breath of wind raises clouds of dust and temperatures climb as high as 50 degrees Celsius (122 degrees Fahrenheit). Thin strips of greenery edging the river are the only signs of life in this barren region. But the Afar Triangle, now so brown and dusty, was once vibrant and alive.

Here, three million years ago, the Awash River flowed through a savanna carpeted with tall grass and crossed with many smaller rivers and streams. The land had once been covered by tropical rainforests, but these were shrinking as the climate dried. The weather and plant life were changing in the region, and living creatures had to adapt or risk extinction. Rainforest apes needed to venture out from the trees, into the open savanna.

Stand Up, Lucy!

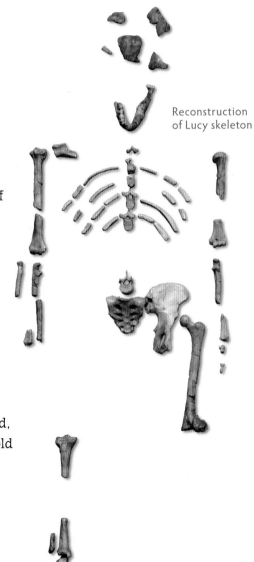

Reconstruction of Lucy skeleton

ON NOVEMBER 30, 1974, Donald Johanson and Tom Gray, two paleoanthropologists (scientists who study the bones of ancient humans and extinct human ancestors), were fossil hunting in the badlands of the Afar desert when one of them spotted something jutting out from a crumbling cliffside. They stopped for a closer look. Sure enough, it was a fossilized bone.

Carefully brushing away the dirt, they soon discovered more bones around it. Johanson and Gray could hardly believe their luck as they realized they'd stumbled upon the skeleton of an ancient hominid (an apelike ancestor of modern humans). When the bones were excavated and studied, they proved to be from a 3.2-million-year-old species of ancient ape that had never been seen before. Johanson named the species *Australopithecus afarensis*, but the little skeleton quickly became famous under another name: Lucy.

One Small Step for Humankind

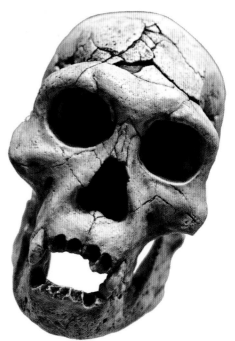

Skull from a bipedal human ancestor

Until Donald Johanson made his incredible discovery, scientists believed the earliest human ancestors had evolved in Asia. Lucy changed all that. Thanks to her, we also know the answer to a key question about how humans evolved—the riddle of which came first, big brains or walking on two legs.

Before Lucy was discovered, many paleoanthropologists had argued that big brains had come first. Apes, they believed, had gradually developed large brains, which helped them to make other important evolutionary changes, such as walking upright and using tools. But Lucy had a very small brain, only about a third of the size of a modern human's, yet her bone structure showed she had walked upright.

So bipedalism—or walking on two legs, rather than four—was the first step for our ape ancestors. And that baby step was taken along the Awash River.

DID YOU BRING YOUR HIP WADERS?

For a time, some scientists thought *Australopithecus* might have begun walking upright to make wading in streams and marshes easier. According to this "aquatic ape" theory, our early human ancestors spent so much time in the water they eventually lost their hairy coats and started to look like modern humans.

Interesting idea—but today, very few paleoanthropologists believe our ancestors were frequent waders. After all, African rivers have always been dangerous places. Hippopotamuses, which still today kill more people each year than any other African animal, lived in those ancient rivers along with snakes, crocodiles, and other deadly creatures. Rivers in Lucy's time were also home to animals we no longer have to worry about, like giant river otters. It just wouldn't have made sense for our ancestors to spend their time in such a risky environment. But we do know the lush vegetation on the riverbanks was an important source of food for *Australopithecus*.

Artist imagining of an *Australopithecus* family defending its territory

The Next Hunt: The First Family

Lucy isn't the only fossilized hominid scientists have found in the Awash River valleys. In 1975, Michael Bush, one of Johanson's students, found the remains of more than 13 hominids, which he called "the First Family."

Because the fossils were found together, we now know that *Australopithecus afarensis* lived in communities or family groups. Bush thinks this group had been gathering food on the riverbank when they were swept away by a flash flood. Their bones, tossed and scattered by the waves, are evidence that rivers have always been a hazard as well as a resource.

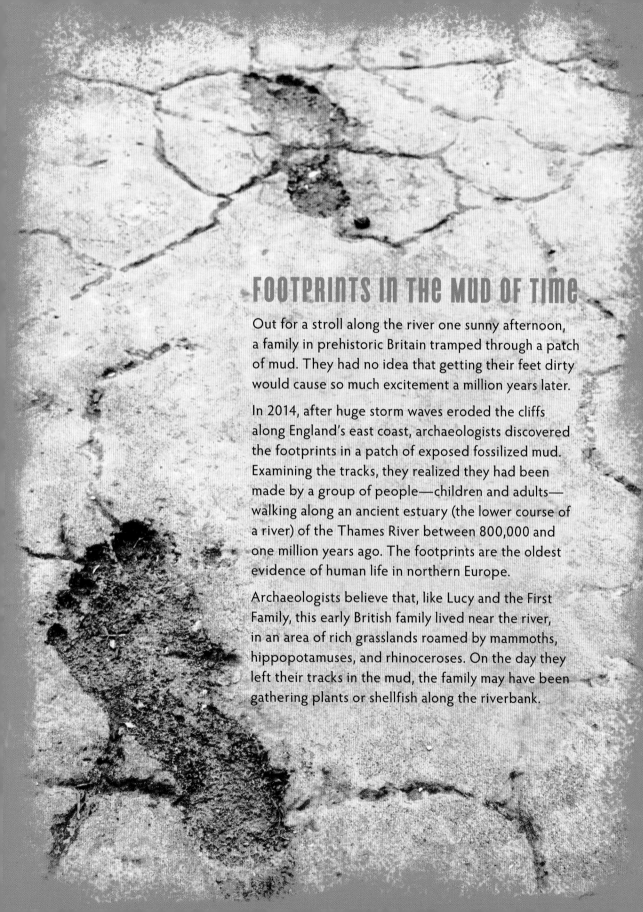

FOOTPRINTS IN THE MUD OF TIME

Out for a stroll along the river one sunny afternoon, a family in prehistoric Britain tramped through a patch of mud. They had no idea that getting their feet dirty would cause so much excitement a million years later.

In 2014, after huge storm waves eroded the cliffs along England's east coast, archaeologists discovered the footprints in a patch of exposed fossilized mud. Examining the tracks, they realized they had been made by a group of people—children and adults—walking along an ancient estuary (the lower course of a river) of the Thames River between 800,000 and one million years ago. The footprints are the oldest evidence of human life in northern Europe.

Archaeologists believe that, like Lucy and the First Family, this early British family lived near the river, in an area of rich grasslands roamed by mammoths, hippopotamuses, and rhinoceroses. On the day they left their tracks in the mud, the family may have been gathering plants or shellfish along the riverbank.

Awash in Fossils

Why is the Awash River Valley such a rich area for fossil hunters? It's part of the East African Rift, which stretches from the Red Sea, off the coast of Egypt, past the southern tip of Lake Malawi in central Africa. A rift is a point where the earth's tectonic plates are pulling apart, creating high volcanic mountains and low valleys.

Most rivers flow out to the ocean, but in the East African Rift the rivers end in lakes at the valley's center. For millions of years, these rivers have carried sediment down to the lakes, gradually burying the bones of animals under layers of earth. As the area dried and the rivers shrank, the layers along the riverbeds were exposed and began to erode, revealing the fossils beneath.

The Awash River isn't as long as the Nile, as wide as the Amazon, as beautiful as the Rhine, or as powerful as the Yangtze. If you saw it, you might think it's kind of insignificant. But you'd be wrong. Because buried along the banks of its dried-up channels is the evidence that can tell us who we are and where we came from: the secret history of human evolution.

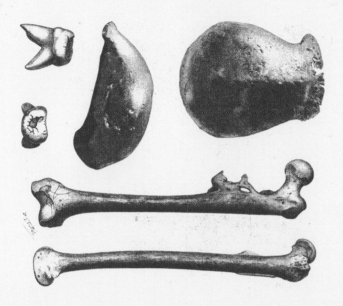

SOLO RIVER, JAVA: RIVER OF THE MISSING LINK

The Awash isn't the only river site where important fossil discoveries have been made. On the island of Java, in Indonesia, a shallow, muddy stream called the Solo River winds its way from the mountains to the coast. Over its long history, the Solo has changed its course many times, and in some places earthquakes have raised up its old riverbed, exposing ancient fossils. In 1891, Eugène Dubois, a Dutch doctor, found a fossilized tooth, a thighbone, and part of a skull in the riverbed. He believed the bones came from the "missing link"—a hominid that proved apes and humans were related. At the time, evolution was still a new and controversial theory, and soon lots of people were talking about the discovery known as Java Man.

Today, the Java Man fossils are classified as *Homo erectus*, a hominid species that lived about 1.5 million years ago. Unlike the now-dry Afar region, Java has a tropical climate that is probably much the same as it was over a million years ago, when *Homo erectus* lived along the Solo River. That makes it easy to imagine what life was like when stegodons (extinct elephant relatives), deer, rhinoceroses, and water buffalo roamed the banks, giant crocodiles lurked in the depths, and *Homo erectus* hunted and gathered food in the fertile lowlands along the river.

2

TIGRIS & EUPHRATES

Twin Rivers of Civilization

NAME

The Sumerian name for the Tigris was *Idiglat* (which means, simply, "river"). The original name of the Euphrates was *Buranum*, or "mighty water source."

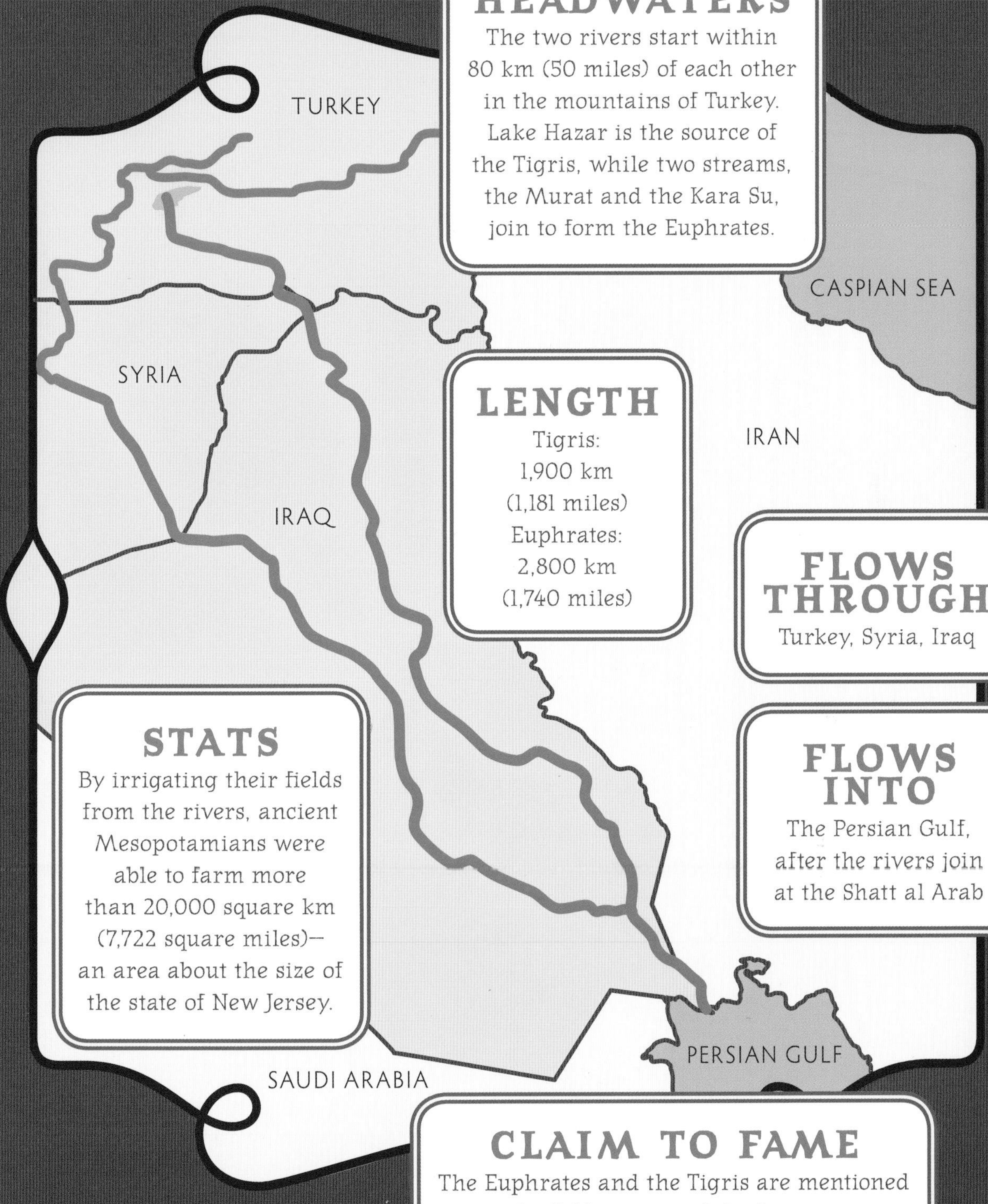

HEADWATERS

The two rivers start within 80 km (50 miles) of each other in the mountains of Turkey. Lake Hazar is the source of the Tigris, while two streams, the Murat and the Kara Su, join to form the Euphrates.

TURKEY

CASPIAN SEA

SYRIA

LENGTH
Tigris:
1,900 km
(1,181 miles)
Euphrates:
2,800 km
(1,740 miles)

IRAN

IRAQ

FLOWS THROUGH
Turkey, Syria, Iraq

STATS

By irrigating their fields from the rivers, ancient Mesopotamians were able to farm more than 20,000 square km (7,722 square miles)— an area about the size of the state of New Jersey.

FLOWS INTO
The Persian Gulf, after the rivers join at the Shatt al Arab

PERSIAN GULF

SAUDI ARABIA

CLAIM TO FAME
The Euphrates and the Tigris are mentioned in the Bible as two of the four rivers that flowed out of the Garden of Eden.

MESOPOTAMIA
[681 BCE]

Adapa, the king's chief engineer, stood tall and proud despite the glare of the harsh noonday sun. Today was the opening of the great royal aqueduct—a moment he'd been working toward for two years, laboring day and night to be sure every detail was perfect. At last, everything was ready. He was confident that not a single drop of the aqueduct's precious liquid would be spilled in its long journey from the river's source in the mountains to the city of Nineveh and its final destination: the magnificent palace gardens. To celebrate Adapa's accomplishment, the king himself was coming.

In the distance, a faint blare of horns and the beating of drums sounded. The royal procession appeared like a mirage on the surface of the river. Dozens of ships, draped in banners, escorted the king's grand barge. As the royal fleet drew near, Adapa could make out a seated figure on the barge's deck—King Sennacherib.

The royal party disembarked, and Adapa and the waiting officials bowed low, carefully keeping their eyes fixed on the ground in the king's presence. Footsteps. A pair of sandaled feet paused in front of Adapa. "Engineer, this is a great day for you. Rise." Adapa stood face to face with his king.

Sennacherib smiled. "I wish you to open the sluice gates and send the waters of the Tigris flowing into Nineveh." He led Adapa to the rope that, with one pull, would let the river waters into the waiting channel and down to the thirsty city.

But first there were speeches, songs to sing, poems to recite, and yet more speeches. The afternoon dragged on. Sennacherib yawned in the shade of his pavilion. Standing patiently in the hot sun, Adapa clung to the rope, waiting for the signal to pull. Finally, his eyes inched shut. For a brief second, as his body sagged with sleep, he pulled the rope, and with a roar the river rushed into the channel.

An appalled silence. Adapa dropped to his knees, waiting to hear his fate. Would he be killed? Cast into slavery?

Then: laughter! "The river gods are eager to test my aqueduct. They cannot wait for speeches today." Could Sennacherib be forgiving him? The sandaled feet appeared again in front of Adapa. When he risked a glance upward, the king winked at him.

Ma'dān boaters in front of reed house, where the Tigris and Euphrates meet

The Story of the Rivers

THE TIGRIS AND EUPHRATES HAVE ALWAYS BEEN TWINS. The sources of these two great rivers are close together in the mountains of Turkey, and as the rivers flow south across Syria and Iraq they are never more than 160 kilometers (99 miles) apart. Because the Tigris is slightly higher than the Euphrates, over the centuries canals have been dug to allow the waters of the Tigris to flow across to its twin river on the other side of Mesopotamia, irrigating the land in between. When they reach the flat plains of Iraq, the rivers slow down, here and there spreading into wide marshes.

The rivers of Mesopotamia (which in ancient Greek means "the land between the rivers") helped to create some of the ancient world's earliest civilizations, among them Sumeria and Babylonia.

The Sumerian civilization produced humankind's first written language, while Babylon was where the first system of laws was written down. Some of the world's first big cities and most powerful empires flourished here from about 5000 to 1600 BCE.

Every year, as snow melted in the mountains of Turkey, water rushed down the rivers, carrying rich silt. When the rivers reached the plains, they flooded their banks, depositing the silt over the fields. In an otherwise harsh, dry region, these annual floods helped to make farming possible.

But the floods could be unreliable, and they didn't happen when farmers needed them most: at the start of the planting season. Instead, the floods were more likely to occur just when farmers were trying to harvest their crops. And because the land was so flat, during the floods the rivers sometimes changed course, stranding farms and even whole villages on brand-new islands or leaving them high and dry, far from the river's new course. The people of Mesopotamia realized early on that to survive in the "land between the rivers," they would need to make wise use of those rivers.

Greening the Desert

MESOPOTAMIAN FARMERS HAD A PROBLEM. Year after year, their fields turned dry and parched, and sometimes the crops withered and died, while nearby the river sailed past. How to get some of that water into their fields? They could haul it in buckets, but that was back-breaking and inefficient. To solve this dilemma, farmers along the Tigris and Euphrates built some of the earliest machines known to humankind. Many farmers still use devices like these to water their fields:

The **shaduf** is built from two upright wooden posts, with a crossbar supporting a long pole. A bucket on a long rope hangs from one end of the pole, and a weight from the other. Pulling down on the rope, farmers dip the bucket in the river, and the weight helps them lift and pour the water into an irrigation channel.

FLOODS: FACT AND FICTION

Many cultures have stories about terrible floods that wipe out almost every living thing. One of the most famous is the story of Noah's Ark in the Christian Bible. According to the story, Noah and his family built a boat, loaded it with two of every kind of animal, and survived a flood of 40 days and 40 nights that destroyed everything else on earth. By the time the rains stopped, the whole world was underwater.

Sound too incredible to be true? The story may have been inspired by actual events. The people of ancient Mesopotamia were the first to tell this story, and archaeological excavations in the Mesopotamian river valleys have found that between 4000 and 2000 BCE there were several terrible floods in the region. Those floods must have seemed like the end of the world to people. But the ship big enough to hold two of every kind of animal? Well, no one has found an ancient Titanic yet!

The **saqiyah** is a large wheel with buckets attached to the edge. Oxen or donkeys turned the wheel and as it revolved, each bucket dipped down into the water, was raised up, and poured out its contents.

Legend has it the **Archimedes screw** was invented by the ancient Greek scientist Archimedes, but it was also used in Mesopotamia. It's a large, hollow pipe, placed on an angle with its lower end in the water. By turning a large screw inside the pipe, the farmer brings the water to the top, where it pours out into an irrigation channel.

A shaduf used in Egypt

Canals: Then and Now

THESE MACHINES WORKED WELL ON A SMALL SCALE, but in ancient Mesopotamia the population was growing fast. People needed to raise more crops to feed the hungry cities. So Mesopotamians put their heads together and came up with an ambitious plan to irrigate the whole region. They built a network of dikes, dams, levees, and canals that directed the waters of the Tigris and the Euphrates where they were needed most—to farms.

People worked together to plan the canal system, and to build it: every canal had to be dug by hand by hundreds of workers. And each canal needed constant care, or it would quickly get choked with silt. "May your canal become clogged with sand!" became a favorite Babylonian curse. But the plan worked: 5,000 years ago

THE TIBER RIVER, ROME: WATER, WATER EVERYWHERE

The ancient Romans were famous builders. Today, all over Europe you can find the remains of Roman buildings, roads, bridges—and aqueducts. These arched brick channels brought clean water into Roman cities, and some are still in use today. It all started with the Tiber River.

For centuries, the people of Rome drank straight from the Tiber River. But as the city grew, a problem developed. Romans were also dumping their sewage into the Tiber, and soon the water was no longer fit to drink. When the city engineers were asked to come up with an answer to the problem, instead of looking for ways to clean the Tiber, they decided to find a new water source. As it turned out, their solution did both.

The Romans built their first aqueduct in 312 BCE. Over the next 500 years, 10 more were added to supply the growing city with clear water from pristine mountain streams. Because the water in the aqueducts ran continuously, Romans had no taps—whatever wasn't used ran into the sewers and out into the Tiber. This meant Rome's sewers were constantly flushed with water, which helped to move the sewage downstream quickly and kept Rome smelling sweet.

the lands of Mesopotamia supported more people than there are today in Iraq, the site of the ancient empire.

Then, slowly, the canals were abandoned, the irrigation channels dried up, and the fields turned to desert. Why? It turns out the Euphrates is what geographers now call an *anastomosing* river—which means it has many channels and streams that are always changing, with some drying up and new ones being formed. When the river changed, it made canals useless and stranded major towns and cities in the desert. Eventually, people gave up. They moved to regions where the rivers were more dependable. If you flew over the area today, you'd still see the outlines of the ancient canals, but on the ground they are invisible—vanished as though these wonders had never been.

Hammurabi's Code

Poor King Hammurabi of Babylon (1792–1750 BCE). There he was, the most powerful man in the kingdom, and how did he get to spend his time? Listening to complaints from his subjects! "My neighbor stole my shaduf, sire," or, "Sire, his canal flooded my field." At last, Hammurabi came up with the world's first written set of laws, and he had them engraved on a giant stone pillar in the middle of Babylon where everyone could see them.

Hammurabi's Code, as the laws are known today, tells us a lot about life in ancient Mesopotamia—including how important it was that water was managed properly. Several laws were very specific about the penalties for mismanaging irrigation works. Such as:

Law 53: "If anyone be too lazy to keep his dam in proper condition, and does not keep it so, if then the dam break and all the fields be flooded, then shall he in whose dam the break occurred be sold for money and the money shall replace the corn which he has caused to be ruined."

Law 55: "If anyone open his ditches to water his crop, but is careless, and the water flood the field of his neighbor, then he shall pay his neighbor corn for his loss."

Law 259: "If anyone steal a waterwheel from the field, he shall pay five shekels in money to its owner."

The Irrigated Gardens of Babylon?

IF YOU LIVED IN A HOT, DRY CITY, what would you dream about? How about a lush, green garden to relax in?

That's just what the Mesopotamians wanted, so they built the most famous garden in history: the Hanging Gardens of Babylon on the shores of the Euphrates. Or so the story goes. There's only

The Hanging Gardens imagined by an artist in 1867

one problem—despite hunting for years, archaeologists have never discovered any evidence of a garden in the ruins of Babylon. Were the hanging gardens just a myth?

Maybe not. Across Mesopotamia from Babylon, in the city of Nineveh, King Sennacherib was determined to have the most wonderful garden ever. To keep his garden lush and green, he built 48 kilometers (30 miles) of channels and aqueducts that brought the water of the Tigris down from high in the mountains. The remains of the aqueducts and the ruins of the palace gardens can still be seen today.

So has the world been mistaken for centuries about the location of the Hanging Gardens—one of the Seven Wonders of the Ancient World? Could be. Sennacherib built Nineveh into such a splendid city it was often called "the New Babylon." That might explain why everyone has been confused about exactly where those fabled gardens actually hung.

LIFE ON THE RIVER: THE SHATT AL ARAB

Before the Tigris and Euphrates reach the Indian Ocean at the Persian Gulf, they join, flowing together to become the Shatt al Arab. Here in southern Iraq, the river broadens into a vast, swampy delta where, among a maze of tiny islands and narrow river channels, the Marsh Arabs, or Ma'dān, live. The Marsh Arabs fish, herd buffalo, and grow rice, but the most important part of their life is harvesting the giant reeds that grow along the riverbanks. The reeds, called qasab, grow to the height of an adult giraffe—up to 6 meters (20 feet) tall. Marsh Arabs use them to build houses, feed their livestock, fuel their fires, and build the reed boats they use to navigate the networks of waterways in the delta. They are truly people of the river.

Ancient village
on Euphrates
River in Turkey

Rivers and Civilization

THANKS TO THE TIGRIS AND THE EUPHRATES, Mesopotamia
became the "cradle of civilization." Some of the world's first cities and
empires arose here, and those early civilizations have shaped and
influenced the ones that came after them—including ours. What would
today's society be like without Hammurabi's legal code, or the discovery
of the principles of engineering that allowed people to build networks of
canals, aqueducts, and irrigation tools? It's possible that our world might
look much different if the rivers of Mesopotamia hadn't pushed people
to invent new ways to make life better in the land between them.

These days, the Tigris and the Euphrates are still testing the limits
of civilization. The rivers flow through countries that are very short of
water, and arguments over who has the right to take water from the
river are getting tense. Will there be wars over water in the future?
Some people think that as the world gets thirstier, it just might happen.
Thousands of years ago, Hammurabi recognized that strong laws were
needed to keep the peace over water rights, and it's still true today.

3

NILE

The Giving River

NAME
The word "Nile" comes from the Greek word *neilos*, meaning river valley. Ancient Egyptians called the river *Iteru*, or "great river."

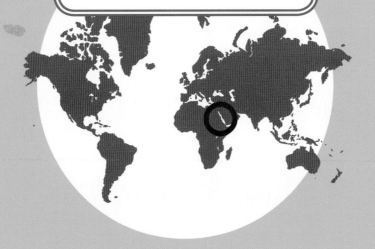

FLOWS INTO
Mediterranean Sea

FLOWS THROUGH
Tanzania, Uganda, Democratic Republic of the Congo, Ethiopia, South Sudan, Sudan, and Egypt, with tributaries in Rwanda, Burundi, Kenya, and Eritrea.

LENGTH
6,737 km
(4,186 miles)

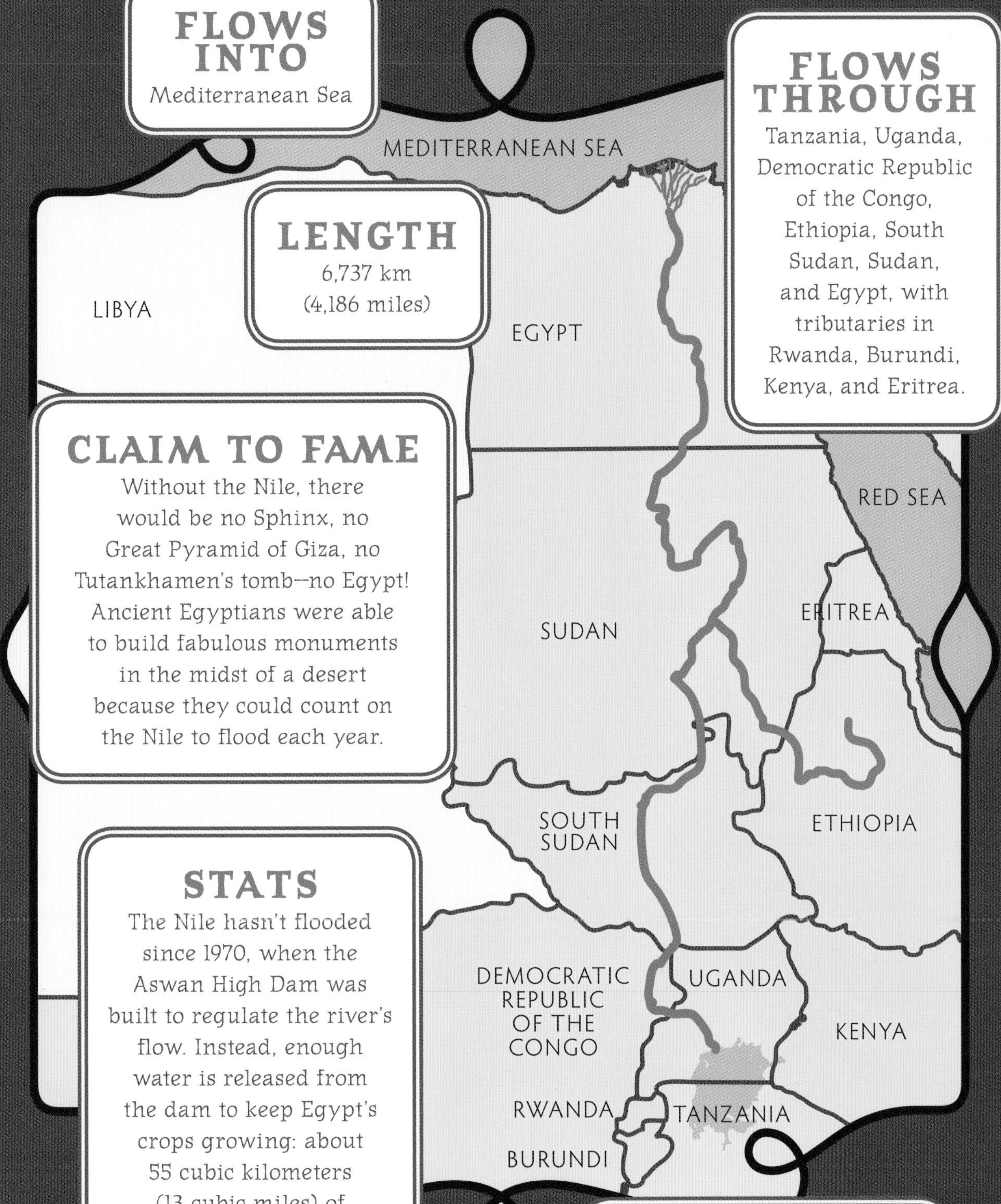

CLAIM TO FAME
Without the Nile, there would be no Sphinx, no Great Pyramid of Giza, no Tutankhamen's tomb—no Egypt! Ancient Egyptians were able to build fabulous monuments in the midst of a desert because they could count on the Nile to flood each year.

STATS
The Nile hasn't flooded since 1970, when the Aswan High Dam was built to regulate the river's flow. Instead, enough water is released from the dam to keep Egypt's crops growing: about 55 cubic kilometers (13 cubic miles) of water every year.

HEADWATERS
Lake Victoria, Tanzania

MEDITERRANEAN SEA

LIBYA

EGYPT

RED SEA

SUDAN

ERITREA

SOUTH SUDAN

ETHIOPIA

DEMOCRATIC REPUBLIC OF THE CONGO

UGANDA

KENYA

RWANDA

TANZANIA

BURUNDI

ASWAN
[2470 BCE]

"Watch out, Akil, I'm coming to get you!"

Neema's dark, wet head bobbed down and disappeared under the water. Seconds later, Akil felt a strong tug on his ankles, and his own head plunged beneath the surface. Underwater, he twisted out of his sister's grasp, turned like a fish, and swam after her, but she was already slicing through the water away from him. When their heads finally popped up above the cool brown water, they were both laughing and gasping for breath.

They'd jumped in for an evening swim in the river. At the end of each long, hot day, the Nile seemed to call to them. They'd race down to the river. "Watch for crocodiles!" their mother's worried voice would float after them, but they hardly paid attention. They'd head for a sheltered bay that kept them out of the current, dive in, and spend the last hour of the day floating and watching the river traffic go by.

Neema paddled up to Akil, lifted a dripping finger, and pointed to the bank: "We won't be able to swim for many more days this summer. Look how high the water is already." Driven into the side of the bank, a tall notched reed was half-submerged in water—a crude nilometer, used to measure the height of the river as it approached its yearly flood. "Soon the fields will be flooded, and we'll have to use a raft to go everywhere. I can't wait!"

Then, from out on the river, they heard voices and the splashing of oars. A fleet of boats glided slowly downriver toward them. The long, narrow crafts rode low in the water, and in the center of each boat rose a huge square mound. Banners fluttered, drummers beat out a rhythm, and the men on board chanted solemnly.

"Neema, those are stone blocks from the quarries up the river, and they're so big it can only mean one thing—Pharaoh Khufu is beginning his pyramid!"

As boat after boat passed before them, Neema and Akil stood motionless in the water, their eyes round with amazement at the might and wealth of the newly crowned pharaoh. He was already starting construction on the vast pyramid that would someday hold his preserved body for the journey to the afterworld.

The Story of the Nile

THE GREAT CIVILIZATION OF ANCIENT EGYPT, which rose around 3,000 BCE, was a bit of a lucky accident. In one of the hottest, driest places on earth, millions of people were able to grow food. It was all because of the Nile. Every summer, when things were at their hottest and driest, the river miraculously surged over its banks and spread water and rich silt over the land. Farmers planted their seeds in the mud, and even though Egypt hardly got any rain, the soaked soil held enough moisture to grow healthy crops each year.

Ancient Egyptians didn't understand why this happened. Why did the Nile never dry up, and why did it flood at the driest time of year? They looked to their gods for reasons, but today we know the answers lie thousands of kilometers to the south:

at the headwaters of the Nile's two branches, the White Nile and the Blue Nile.

The White Nile is born in the tropical rainforests of Burundi, Africa, which receive lots of rain all year long. Then, on its way down to Egypt, the White Nile passes through a number of large lakes. The White Nile's steady supply of rainwater and lakewater ensures that the Egyptian Nile never runs dry.

The Blue Nile, on the other hand, has its source in the Ethiopian highlands, which receive a large amount of rain just once a year, between May and October. During these five months, more than 150 centimeters (60 inches) of rain falls. That's about the height of a small adult, and all that water washing into the river increased its flow dramatically. Each year when the swollen Nile reached the flatlands of the Egyptian delta, the river would overflow its banks and flood the waiting fields.

NILE TIME

The Nile floods were so dependable, and so essential, that the ancient Egyptians named their seasons after the changes in the river's flow, dividing their calendar into *akhet* (flood season), *peret* (growing season), and *shemu* (drought season). During *akhet*, from July to October, the land was flooded and people fished, mended tools, and waited for the water to recede so they could plant their crops. Farming took place from October to February. And in the yearly drought, from March to June, everyone worked to build and repair irrigation ditches and reservoirs for the next season's rushing river waters.

My, You've Grown!

BECAUSE THE ANNUAL FLOODS OCCURRED SO REGULARLY, Egyptians were able to forecast the year's harvest by measuring the height of the river. They knew if the flooding was lower than usual, the crops would suffer. And if the floods were too high? That could also hurt the harvest—the crops might drown in the waterlogged fields.

Each year, government officials kept watch on the rise of the river at several official *nilometers* along the course of the Nile. Like giant measuring sticks, these were pillars positioned at strategic points on the river. Each nilometer was marked off in cubits, an ancient measurement based on the length of a human arm from elbow to fingertip. In an average year, the Nile would rise to a height of 16 cubits during its flood.

Egyptian girls with nilometers visible on rocks, around 1910

Nile News

How high is the water today? Will it be a good year? Everyone in Egypt wanted to hear about the water level in the Nile, so town criers walked the streets loudly announcing the daily rise. If the water was high, it was a sign the gods were favoring Egypt. But if the river was low, the people knew they had offended the gods somehow.

Measuring the height of the floodwaters wasn't done just to tell people how well crops would grow—the government used the information to determine that year's tax rate. (The Egyptians were the first people in the world to pay taxes.) If the water rose to 16 cubits, there would be a good harvest, so the government would demand high taxes. If the rains failed at the headwaters of the Blue Nile, the floodwaters would be lower and the tax collectors would have to reduce taxes, because farmers would earn less. An exceptionally low Nile meant the crops would shrivel and the harvest would fail, bringing famine to the people and no taxes for the pharaoh.

River Transport

All those taxes made the Egyptian pharaohs very wealthy. So what did they do with their money? Invested it in the afterlife, of course.

The planning for a pharaoh's pyramid—the monument where his body would be entombed after his death—began in the very first years of his reign. These massive burial structures could take up to 30 years to complete and required thousands of workers each year. And like much else in Egypt, without the Nile River, they would not have been possible at all.

The stone for the pyramids came from quarries near Aswan, in the south of Egypt. Each enormous stone block could weigh as much as nine elephants. Dragging them over hundreds of kilometers of sandy desert to the building sites in the north of the country was clearly not an option. The solution was to wait until the Nile's annual flooding, between July and October.

Workers dug canals so that boats could sail right up to the pyramid sites. Then, when the Nile floodwaters filled the canals with water, the workers loaded the massive granite blocks onto reed barges and floated them 800 kilometers (almost 500 miles) downstream to the pyramids. While they reduced the labor involved in transporting the building blocks, the canals were mighty undertakings in themselves. It's estimated it took 100,000 men 10 years to build the canal from the Nile to the Great Pyramid of Giza.

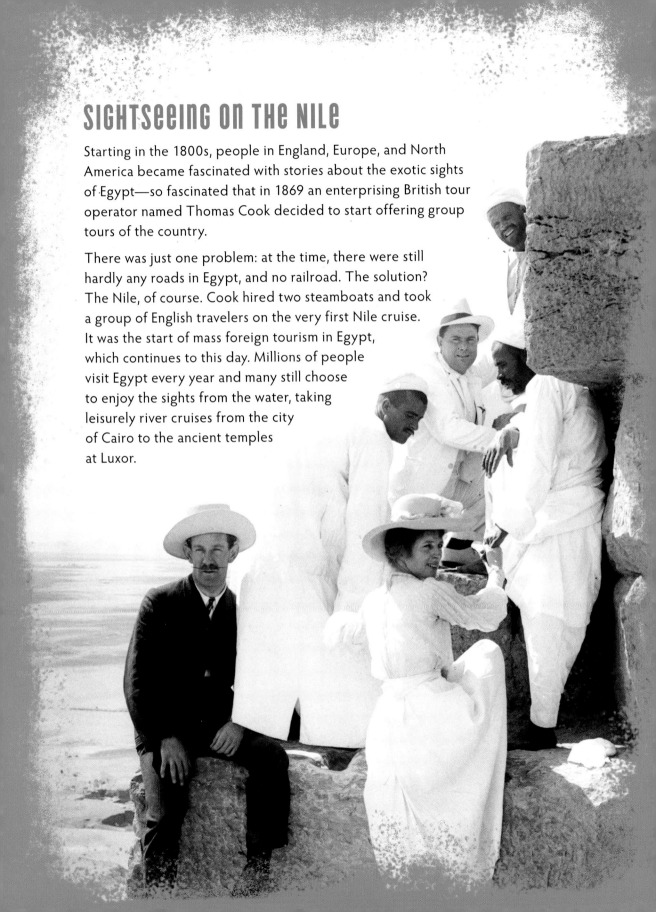

SIGHTSEEING ON THE NILE

Starting in the 1800s, people in England, Europe, and North America became fascinated with stories about the exotic sights of Egypt—so fascinated that in 1869 an enterprising British tour operator named Thomas Cook decided to start offering group tours of the country.

There was just one problem: at the time, there were still hardly any roads in Egypt, and no railroad. The solution? The Nile, of course. Cook hired two steamboats and took a group of English travelers on the very first Nile cruise. It was the start of mass foreign tourism in Egypt, which continues to this day. Millions of people visit Egypt every year and many still choose to enjoy the sights from the water, taking leisurely river cruises from the city of Cairo to the ancient temples at Luxor.

A River Civilization

Pyramids, sphinxes, mummies—all the things that say "Egypt" to us today were gifts of the Nile. Learning how to use the river and take advantage of its annual floods was the greatest triumph of ancient Egyptian civilization.

In the 20th century, Egyptians built one of the world's biggest dams, the Aswan Dam, to control the Nile's floods. Today, the river's waters are contained in Lake Nasser, a man-made reservoir behind the dam. Throughout the year, enough water is released to irrigate the land. But the rich silt that used to wash down the river and into the fields, nourishing the crops, is trapped behind the dam. Without it, farmers have to use chemical fertilizers on their land, which seep into the river and are carried into the Mediterranean Sea. Scientists and environmentalists are working to understand the effects of the dam on the Nile's ecology, and to find ways to restore the river, and the lands it waters, to a more natural state.

The Aswan Dam

THE INDUS RIVER, PAKISTAN: FIGHT THE FLOOD!

The ancient river-based cultures of Egypt and Mesopotamia are famous. But did you know there were also ancient cities in today's Pakistan? As long ago as 2600 BCE there were hundreds of villages and at least two major cities along the Indus River, which runs from the high Himalayan mountains down to the Indian Ocean. Archaeologists call this ancient culture the Harappan Empire.

The empire's two chief cities, Harappa and Mohenjodaro, were extremely sophisticated. Filled with houses built of brick, they had large public baths and the world's first indoor plumbing. The river was the people's highway, bringing wood from the Himalayas and food from the farms upstream, but it was also their curse. The cities flooded so frequently, the Harappans built city walls up to 1.5 meters (5 feet) thick to try to keep the river out.

Eventually, the floods and other environmental changes drove the Harappans away. Archaeologists think an earthquake caused the Indus River to change its course, sending it down hillsides the Harappans had logged. The bare hillsides caused the river to run faster, flood more frequently, and create more damage. Before long, the vast cities were abandoned, and the Harappan culture vanished as though it had never been.

4

RHINE

An International River

FLOWS THROUGH
Switzerland, Liechtenstein, Austria, Germany, France, the Netherlands

FLOWS INTO
The North Sea

LENGTH
1,390 km (864 miles)

THE NORTH SEA

THE NETHERLANDS

BELGIUM

LUXEMBOURG

GERMANY

FRANCE

LIECHTENSTEIN   AUSTRIA

SWITZERLAND

STATS
The Rhine carries more commercial traffic than any other river on earth—about 228 million metric tons (251 million short tons) of goods are shipped on the river every year.

HEADWATERS
Rheinwaldhorn Glacier, Swiss Alps

CLAIM TO FAME
The Rhine's beauty has inspired artists and poets for centuries. The river flows past thick forests, steep mountains, stone castles and villages, lonely towers, and even an enchanted rock—at least, according to local legend. In the legend, a beautiful maiden inhabits the rock known as the Lorelei. Her singing lures sailors closer until they are dashed to death on the rock. Perched on the cliffs and riverbanks around the Lorelei are nearly 30 ruined castles—so although you may not believe the legend of the rock, you can still feel as though you're in a fairytale.

ALONG THE RHINE RIVER
[1255]

Franz was at the bow, his eyes scanning the waters ahead for rocks, when he spotted something unusual. "Chain!" he shouted, scrambling to join the others on the deck of their wide-bottomed merchant ship. By the time he reached the deck, the others had reacted to his warning. Karl and Pieter were manning the oars and pulling back hard to slow the ship. Otto was hastily lowering the large square sail.

Captain Hessler paced the small deck beside the open hold and cursed his luck. "This is not a licensed river toll—the lord of this castle has no right to stop my ship! Do these princes think there is no law along the river?"

As the captain fumed, the merchant ship drifted toward the heavy iron chain spanning the river. One end of the chain was linked to the walls of a forbidding stone castle, while the other end was bolted into the cliffs across the narrow river channel. A small boat had pushed off from shore, and soon it came alongside them.

"By the order of Baron Werner von Bolanden, prince of this castle of Ingelheim, if you wish to proceed you must pay a toll of 20 silver denarii. If you do not pay, we will board your ship and claim it and your cargo for our lord." The speaker was a small man, but behind him stood three others with their bows trained on the men of Captain Hessler's ship. More archers lined the cliff tops and the castle walls. Franz and his shipmates were trapped. In this narrow gorge, ships were at the mercy of whoever controlled the riverside, and clearly the baron had decided to take advantage of his castle's position.

Captain Hessler was outraged. "Twenty denarii? That's more than double the lawful toll! Your master is a Raubritter—a robber baron."

Thunk! An arrow buried itself deeply in the wooden mast beside Hessler's head. The captain's shoulders sagged with defeat. "Get the money chest, boy. We must pay these men today, but one day we will make them pay."

Franz looked at the small pile of silver in the bottom of the captain's money chest and wondered how many more castles they had to pass on their journey up the Rhine. Would they make it?

Stahleck Castle, built around 1135

The Story of the Rhine

THE ICY WATERS OF THE RHINE surge out of a glacier high
up in the Alps. The river churns and froths through deep mountain
gorges until it reaches Switzerland's Lake Constance. From there,
it slows slightly, but it is still a fast-moving river, cutting through
steep-sided valleys as it passes through Germany's Black Forest and
the steep terraced hillsides of the Middle Rhine, which are dotted
with castles and quaint villages.

By the time it reaches the wide, marshy plains of the Netherlands,
the river has become slower and broader. It arrives at the North Sea
near the city of Rotterdam, Europe's busiest port. Here, oceangoing
transport ships enter and leave the river, moving cargo of every
description into and out of Europe.

The millions of people who live along the Rhine, in Germany and France and Switzerland, have always depended on the river. It's been an essential trade route linking northern and southern Europe for centuries. Without it, mountainous, landlocked Switzerland would have been almost cut off from the rest of the world until the development of railroads, paved roads, and cars.

But sharing a busy river among many countries hasn't always been easy. Whoever controls the river holds a lot of power, and over the centuries wars have been fought, alliances formed, treaties signed and then broken, as each country along the Rhine struggled to make sure it got its share of the river's wealth.

River of Ages

Roman bridge over the Rhine

AMONG THE EARLIEST INHABITANTS along the Rhine were the Neanderthals, named after the Rhine's Neander Valley, where the bones of these extinct human cousins were first discovered. Thirty thousand years ago, Neanderthals hunted woolly mammoths and rhinoceroses in the open tundra beside the Rhine, and sheltered in caves along the steep-sided river valleys. When modern humans replaced Neanderthals as the dominant human species, they too were drawn to the fertile valleys of the Rhine.

Ancient Celts gave the river its name as early as 600 BCE. When the Romans arrived at the banks of the Rhine, more than 2,000 years ago, they found at least seven Celtic and Germanic tribes already sharing the stream, using it to communicate and trade with each other. The river became the eastern boundary of the Roman Empire.

Eltz castle, built in the 1100s

My River! No, Mine!

W<small>HEN THE</small> R<small>OMAN</small> E<small>MPIRE</small> disintegrated in the fifth century CE, the Rhine was up for grabs. Within 100 years, the land along the river had been carved up into 97 tiny states—each led by a prince or duke, and each claiming rights to the river. There were fierce battles over the best fishing holes, and feuding villages tore down each other's dams.

Most of all, the princes warred over the right to charge ships for using "their" part of the river. They built castles and towers along the banks and stopped every ship, demanding money before they would let each one past their castle walls.

Take a Right on Church Street

I<small>N</small> 800 CE, C<small>HARLEMAGNE</small>, the king of the Franks, was crowned the first Holy Roman Emperor. The Holy Roman Empire would control central Europe, and the Rhine, for most of the next eight centuries. Emperors made the river safe for merchants by decreeing that only princes and archbishops with their permission could demand money from passing ships. Soon, the Rhine became known as Church Street, because so many archbishops built castles along the river. Official tollbooths had to be at least 5 kilometers (3 miles) apart, and the emperor stationed soldiers along the river to protect ships from attack. As a result, taking a ship up or down the river got less expensive and less dangerous. Trade increased, and everyone prospered.

Then, abruptly, the whole system collapsed. Holy Roman Emperor Frederick II died in 1250 CE and no other king in Europe was powerful enough to take his place as Emperor. For the next 20 years, while kings and princes squabbled over who would rule Europe, no one was watching the Rhine. Renegade princes started building towers and castles on the riverbanks to demand money from passing ships—even stretching iron chains across the river to make sure no ships got through without paying. These new lords of the river, known as robber barons, weren't above piracy either. They sometimes seized entire ships, or kidnapped passengers and demanded outrageous ransoms. Everyone sailing on the Rhine was at risk from these medieval bullies. Clearly, something had to be done, or soon all trade on the river would stop.

THE COST OF DOING RIVER BUSINESS

In the 13th century, the standard Rhine toll for an average ship was 8 denarii. The denarius was a silver coin used throughout the Holy Roman Empire. Each denarius contained just over half a gram (0.02 ounces) of pure silver. In today's prices, that's only about 50 cents U.S., so each toll was about the equivalent today of 4 dollars. At the time, that was a lot of money: a single denarius could buy 50 peaches in the markets of Paris.

Merchant ships also occasionally paid tolls in cargo: mainly lead, copper, wine, or slaves. These in-kind tolls tended to be much more expensive for the ships' owners, so it's likely the owners only paid for tolls with cargo when they were forced to do so.

FACT OR FICTION? THE MOUSE TOWER OF THE RHINE

On a small island in the Rhine stands a stone tower with a terrifying legend—the Mäuseturm, or Mouse Tower. Hatto II, the Archbishop of Mainz, built the tower in 968 CE in order to rob passing boats, and it soon made him rich. Then, the legend goes, famine struck the nearby villages. Peasants came to Hatto begging for some of the grain stored in his barns. Instead, Hatto locked them in an empty barn and set it on fire, taunting, "Hear the mice squeak!" as they shouted for help.

That night, when Hatto returned to his castle, he was attacked by an army of mice. He tried to hide in his tower, but the mice chewed through the wooden doors and climbed to the top of the tower, where they ate the evil bishop alive.

There's no evidence the real Hatto ever locked peasants in a burning barn or that he was nibbled to death by mice. But the legend is proof of just how hated and feared the greedy robber barons of the Rhine were throughout the Middle Ages.

Call the Rhine League!

In 1254, THE LAW-ABIDING PRINCES banded together to bring order back to the Rhine. They formed the *Rheinischer Bund*, or Rhine League, and their mission was to put the robber barons out of business. They cobbled together an army and attacked the castles of the outlaw barons. Although they didn't win every battle, over the next three years the Rhine League successfully destroyed more than a dozen castles.

Rare was the robber baron who could withstand the Rhine League, but there was at least one who emerged victorious from a skirmish. In 1255, Diether von Katzenelnbogen, the owner of Castle Rheinfels, broke the law by raising his river tolls. Twenty-six towns in the Rhine League brought their armies together against Diether: 8,000 foot soldiers, 1,000 cavalry, and 50 ships laid siege to Castle Rheinfels. The siege lasted for a year and 14 weeks, until the League finally gave up, declaring Diether's castle invulnerable.

Fortunately, there weren't many castles as well-defended as Rheinfels, and eventually, thanks to the Rhine League's vigilance, ships could safely return to the river.

save our queen

The Rhine League was formed to make the Rhine safe for river traffic. But the league did other good deeds, including rescuing the kidnapped Queen of Holland. In 1255, William II of Holland and his wife, Elisabeth of Brunswick-Luneburg, were visiting a neighboring prince when Elisabeth was abducted by a notorious robber baron, the Baron Herman von Rietburg. He locked her up in his castle on the Rhine and demanded a huge ransom for her release. The king, unable to pay the fortune, turned to the Rhine League for help. The League's armies surrounded the baron's castle, and after a long siege, he was forced to release the captive queen.

Working Together to Bring the River Back

THE RHINE—"yesterday a line of battle, tomorrow the bond of union." That's what Charles de Gaulle, the president of France, predicted just after the Second World War. Countries that had fought each other bitterly for control of the Rhine now had to work together again. During the war, it had been too dangerous to ship goods along the Rhine, but with the fighting over, cargo ships could return to the river, and former enemies would need to make new agreements to regulate the trade along it.

De Gaulle was right. Within a few years, the Rhine was again one of the busiest commercial waterways in the world—and it still is. An incredible number of ships pass up and down it each year, and the countries along its banks work together to keep the river traffic flowing, as well as to keep the river clean. Today, through the Rhine Commission, Germany, France, and the Netherlands are cooperating in efforts to protect and restore the river's environment.

THE LAMARI RIVER: WATERY DIVIDER

While the Rhine has been connecting Europe for thousands of years, rivers can also divide cultures. The Lamari River in the highlands of New Guinea rushes through a deep, steep-sided valley. For centuries, the Fore people lived on one side of the river, while across the river were the villages of the Anga. Although the two tribes didn't live far apart, the river kept them isolated. When anthropologists arrived in their villages, in the 1930s, they were surprised to find the Fore and the Anga spoke different languages and had very different cultures. While the Anga were warlike, living in villages defended by high spiked walls, the Fore were peaceful gardeners, raising sweet potatoes and pigs in their settlements.

The Lamari is an example of a river as a natural barrier, something countries often take advantage of when deciding on borders. Today, rivers form part of the borders for many countries, including between Mexico and the U.S. (the Rio Grande), between India and Pakistan (the Indus), and between Thailand and Laos (the Mekong).

5

AMAZON

A World of Water

NAME

Spanish explorers named the river after the Amazons, legendary female warriors from Greek myth who they believed lived along its course.

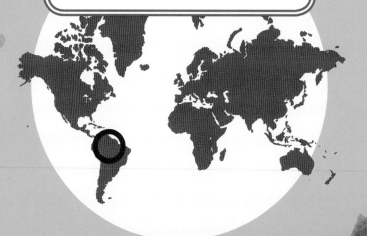

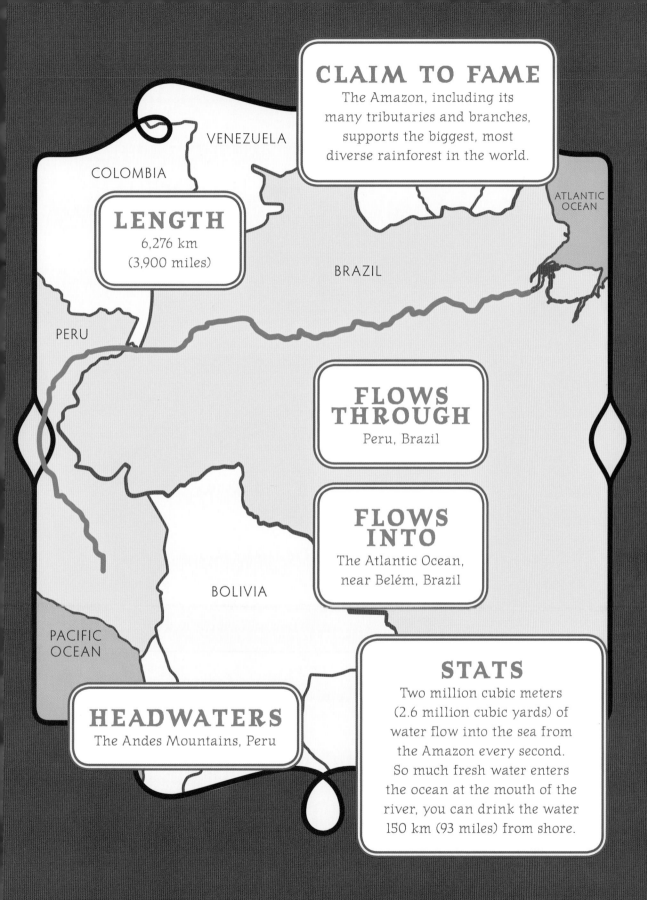

CLAIM TO FAME
The Amazon, including its many tributaries and branches, supports the biggest, most diverse rainforest in the world.

VENEZUELA

COLOMBIA

ATLANTIC OCEAN

LENGTH
6,276 km
(3,900 miles)

BRAZIL

PERU

FLOWS THROUGH
Peru, Brazil

FLOWS INTO
The Atlantic Ocean, near Belém, Brazil

BOLIVIA

PACIFIC OCEAN

STATS
Two million cubic meters (2.6 million cubic yards) of water flow into the sea from the Amazon every second. So much fresh water enters the ocean at the mouth of the river, you can drink the water 150 km (93 miles) from shore.

HEADWATERS
The Andes Mountains, Peru

OUTSIDE MANAUS, BRAZIL
[2014]

Maria woke up early. Inside her family's home, it was still dark, but outside the sun was glinting on the surface of the river. It was the best time of day, when the mist was rising from the water and the birds and monkeys called to one another along the riverbanks. In a few hours, the heat would deaden the air, and the only noise would be the buzz of insects. It was time to be on the river.

She pulled on her clothes and in a few minutes she was climbing down the ladder from her family's stilt house and picking her way across the muddy ground toward the riverbank. Her father's dugout canoe had been pulled high up on the bank and lashed to a palm tree to keep it from floating away in the night. It was heavy, but with a few strong tugs she slid it down into the water. She grabbed a paddle and a fishing net and jumped in. Her parents didn't like her out on the river alone, and her grandmother muttered that in her day no girl would go fishing, but Maria loved the river.

Soon she was well out in the stream, paddling against the current up to her favorite fishing spot. No one was stirring yet at the homes of their neighbors. Each stilt house was quiet and shuttered. There were no other river people, or ribereños, out yet.

In a quiet backwater of the river, she stopped paddling and took out her fishing net and pole, scanning the dark water for shapes of fish. A shadow flicked by under the canoe, then another and another—it might be a school of pacu, small, tasty, red-bellied fish. Maria was about to throw her net over when something bumped the canoe, rocking it wildly. She grabbed at the sides of the lurching boat to stop herself from pitching over into the water.

She was looking around in panic—was it a caiman? a snake?—when a loud snort alerted her, and she spotted a wide pink back rising from the water nearby. She laughed with relief. It was only a boto, one of the pink river dolphins, being playful or curious. "Go away!" she ordered, splashing her paddle in the water. "You'll scare off my breakfast!"

The Rio Negro (black river) meets the reddish Rio Solimões in the upper Amazon

The Story of the Amazon

THE AMAZON IS THE GREATEST of all the earth's rivers.
Running from the high Andes Mountains down to the Atlantic Ocean,
the Amazon accounts for nearly five percent of the world's fresh water.
But is it one river, or many?

The Amazon has a staggering 1,100 tributaries and an uncountable
number of river channels. Those rivers widen into thousands of lakes,
and every year for months at a time the Amazon floods hundreds of
kilometers of tropical forest. Sometimes the forests are drowned under
13 meters (43 feet) of water. South America sinks by 8 centimeters
(3 inches) every year because of the extra weight of all that floodwater!

The animal and plant life in the region has adapted to the
unusually fluid conditions. Some trees depend on fish to distribute

their seeds, while some fish species eat fruit. The Amazon delta is one of the most diverse regions on our planet.

Until the first Spanish ship turned up at the mouth of the Amazon in 1500, this watery wonderland was inhabited by many different aboriginal groups, including some that had developed large civilizations. No one knows how many aboriginal people lived along the Amazon, but we do know that over the next several centuries many thousands died. They were killed in battles and uprisings against the Spanish, died of diseases introduced from Europe, or simply fled into the remote jungle to escape the invaders.

Despite this, there are a few areas along the Amazon where people still live much as they did before the arrival of Europeans. Others, called *ribereños*, or river people, have adapted to some of the advantages of modern life but still live in close connection with the river, fishing and hunting along its banks and raising gardens in the fertile soil of the floodplains.

Scientists estimate that the lush, watery world created by the Amazon contains one-tenth of all the plant and animal species in the world. On a boat ride through the Amazon delta, you'd pass endless tropical trees heavy with sweet fruit or festooned with scented flowers. Vines, creepers, and strangler plants would wind up the smooth trunks of every tree. Brazil nut trees. Silk cotton trees. Walking palms. Murumuru palms. Big-leaf mahogany trees. And trees that ooze a white, sticky sap: rubber trees.

BACKWARD AND FORWARD

Today, the Amazon River flows eastward from the Andes Mountains of Peru down to the Atlantic Ocean. But did you know it used to flow in the opposite direction?

Geologists tell us that millions of years ago, the river ran west, emptying into the Pacific Ocean. Then, about 65 million years ago, at the end of the Cretaceous period, the Andes Mountains started growing higher. Water can't flow uphill, so the river flipped and cut a new course down to the east. Now *that's* changing the world!

Amazonian Indians slashed the bark of the trees they called "weeping trees," collecting the sap in palm leaves and molding the white latex into sheets and capes to protect themselves from the rain. By the 1800s Europeans had realized how much money could be made from these trees, and the rubber boom was on. The town of Manaus, a sleepy little river port on the Amazon in the heart of the rubber-growing region, changed almost overnight into a rowdy boomtown where rubber millionaires lit their cigars with 100-dollar bills and gave their horses buckets of champagne to drink.

Rubber trees are only one of the miraculous plants of the Amazon. The fruit of the wild camu camu tree has more vitamin C than oranges, the palm trees known as "living oil factories" produce more oil than olive trees, and the leaves of the stevia bush are 300 times sweeter than table sugar. So far, only a few of these plants have been grown commercially.

Collecting the Amazon

ALFRED RUSSEL WALLACE was a young English surveyor who had a passion for insects, birds, plants, and fish. In 1848, at the age of 25, he saved enough money to pay for his passage to Brazil, where he started a new life as a professional collector. For four years, he paddled up and down the Amazon River and its tributaries, gathering specimens of every unusual plant and animal he came across.

In those four years, he was stung by wasps and hornets, bitten by fire ants and poisonous caterpillars, nearly drowned in river rapids, threatened by caimans (large reptiles in the alligator family) and hostile indigenous tribes, and almost killed by malaria. But he kept going, mapping the many channels and streams of the Amazon, taking detailed notes on everything he saw and making precise drawings of the plant and animal life of the rivers and forest.

Then, as Wallace was returning to England with the specimens he'd collected along the river, disaster struck. His ship caught fire while crossing the Atlantic, destroying his collection, his notes, his journals, and his drawings—everything he'd worked on for four long years. Wallace was able to save just one small tin box containing a few sketches of the Amazon River fish he'd observed.

Wallace barely escaped with his life. He floated in a lifeboat with other survivors for days, until they were picked up by another ship. He returned to England penniless, so he accepted the first job he was offered—a job that took him across the world again, to Malaysia.

The diverse wildlife around the Amazon includes these poisonous caterpillars

There, Wallace continued collecting new species for another eight years. Finally, one day Wallace had an inspiration: he realized how the many different species of birds and animals he'd observed had developed their specialized characteristics. The strongest individuals seemed to have reproduced most successfully, passing on their strengths to their offspring. Generation by generation, the new traits took hold. In 1858 he wrote a long letter about his new idea to a friend back in England—Charles Darwin.

Learning to Look Closely

WHILE IN THE AMAZON, Wallace had often noticed how a particular species of plant or animal might be confined to just one tributary of the Amazon. The more he thought about it, the more he became convinced that the reason for the astonishing variety of wildlife in the Amazon delta was that the animals and plants had been isolated by the maze of rivers. In time, through a series of tiny changes passed down from parent to offspring, they had developed unique characteristics that helped them survive in their specific environment. Wallace's idea is now known as the theory of natural selection, and it is key to the modern science of evolutionary biology.

A FISHY TALE

The Amazon River and its tributaries are home to 3,000 species of freshwater fish. At least, that's how many have been observed and named so far. It is estimated there may be up to 6,000 more species waiting to be discovered in the deep, dark waters of the Amazon.

Ever since Darwin's return from his voyage to the Galápagos
Islands on the ship *Beagle,* he'd been thinking the same thing:
animals change over time through a process of natural selection.
But he'd never gotten around to publishing his theories—yet.
When he read Wallace's letter, he realized that if he didn't act fast,
Wallace would beat him to it. That same year, Darwin presented his
theory, along with Wallace's letter, to an audience of Britain's most
distinguished scientists. The following year, he published his famous
book about natural selection, called *On the Origin of Species.*

The theory of natural selection was one of the most controversial
ideas in the entire history of science. The idea that animals (including
humans!) changed over time stunned people and it rocked the foun-
dations of religious belief. But Wallace knew it was true, because he
had seen for himself those tiny differences in Amazonian fish, insects,
and birds. The tin box he'd saved from the fire, with his incredibly
detailed drawings of fish, perfectly illustrated the revolutionary new
theory. Science would never be the same.

The Amazon Today

Without the plants of South and Central America, the world would have no chocolate, no pineapples, potatoes, chilies, corn, or tomatoes. In the rainforest today, there are very likely plants waiting to be discovered that can heal us, feed us, or build our economies in unimagined ways. But we are starting to understand that in order to take advantage of the gifts of the Amazon, we have to learn how to sustain the environment of the Amazon.

Many people know that the Amazon rainforests are threatened by logging. But the river is also in danger—pollution from mines, cattle ranches, oil wells, and logging operations flows into the Amazon and is endangering the fish and wildlife that depend on the river. Meanwhile, dams planned for the river could disrupt the flooding that nourishes the world's biggest rainforest. The good news? People in South America and all over the world are working together to protect the river and its vast forests, realizing that without the Amazon, a whole world of possibilities will vanish.

Pollution on the Amazon River

THE MURRAY RIVER: ABORIGINAL HOMELAND

Like the Amazon, Australia's Murray River was a lifeline for the aboriginal peoples who made the area their home for thousands of years. We don't know exactly how many people lived along the Murray River, but it was likely one of the most highly populated areas of Australia. Aboriginal peoples built canoes and rafts from the bark of the red gum trees that grew on the riverbanks, wove fishing nets from the reeds that filled the shallows, gathered crayfish and mussels, and dug for tasty bulrush roots on the banks.

When European settlers arrived on the banks of the Murray, they saw the river's value too. The rich lands along the Murray were perfect for farming. Soon, aboriginal people were forced from their settlements along the river to make way for farms and ranches. The settlers planted the same crops they'd raised in England—crops that needed a lot of irrigation in the dry Australian air. They tried to raise livestock—cows and pigs—and those needed a lot of water too. Cities and towns sprang up, taking more and more of the Murray's water. Pretty soon, the river was running dry.

Today, Australians are looking for ways to restore the health of the Murray River. They are remembering the indigenous peoples' traditional ways of living on the river, and realizing that indigenous people need to be part of deciding the future of the Murray. A lot of people depend on the Murray River today—and the Murray depends on people, who must find ways to manage the river responsibly so it survives for the future.

6

ZAMBEZI

Exploring the River of Freedom

NAME
Zambezi means "great river" in Bantu, the language of the Tonga people.

HEADWATERS
Northwestern Zambia

STATS
Portuguese explorer Vasco da Gama was the first European to see the Zambezi River. He called it *Rio dos Bons Sinais,* or "River of Good Omens."

DEMOCRATIC
REPUBLIC
OF THE CONGO

ANGOLA

LENGTH
2,574 km
(1,599 miles)

ZAMBIA

MALAWI

ZIMBABWE

NAMIBIA   BOTSWANA

MOZAMBIQUE

FLOWS THROUGH
Zambia, Angola, Botswana, Namibia, Zimbabwe, Mozambique

FLOWS INTO
The Indian Ocean

INDIAN
OCEAN

CLAIM TO FAME
The world's biggest waterfall, Victoria Falls, is on the Zambezi River. The falls on the Zambezi are twice the height and width of Niagara Falls.

ZAMBEZI RIVER
[NOVEMBER 1855]

The river was wide, calm, and flat, dotted with small islands. Trees crowded the banks—palmyras, date palms, dark green motsouri trees. Overhead arched a vast and cloudless sky. The air was very still.

Suddenly the silence was broken by the splash of paddles. Canoes slid into sight, filled with young African men paddling steadily. In the middle of the first canoe was a slumped figure, paler than the rest. He wasn't paddling.

The canoes headed for the riverbank, beaching on a flat strip of ground. The men sprang out of the boats. One extended a helping hand to the pale man.

David Livingstone took his friend's hand. "Mpepe, I am so sick. I don't think I can make it all the way to the ocean. This river is much longer than I had expected."

Mpepe smiled encouragingly. "Dr. Livingstone, I promised my chief I would see you safely to the end of this journey, and I will. The river is dangerous, filled with hippos and crocodiles that will try to overturn our canoes, but we're all experienced boatmen. And soon you'll see something that you'll never forget ... look."

Far in the distance, Livingstone could see a tiny white plume against the blue horizon. He heard a faint murmur, which grew to a loud roar as they traveled downstream. What lay ahead?

The next day, the roar was deafening, and huge columns of white spray rose like smoke into the air. Mpepe guided the canoes to an island in the middle of the stream. Clambering out, the men inched cautiously onto the rocks until, raising his hand, Mpepe warned them to go no further. Livingstone looked down.

He was perched on the very edge of a giant cliff. On either side of him, the river crashed straight down hundreds of feet into a rocky gorge, throwing up billowing clouds of froth.

"What is this place, Mpepe?"

"Mosi-oa-Tunya—the smoke that thunders."

Thanks to his guides, David Livingstone was the first European to visit the world's biggest waterfall, which he called Victoria Falls.

The Story of the Zambezi

THE ZAMBEZI RIVER COMES TO LIFE in the high wetland plateau of Zambia, in a type of grassy swamp unique to central Africa called a *dambo*. Dambos absorb the rain that falls during the rainy season, releasing it slowly all year long as rivers or streams.

The Zambezi is broad, shallow, and slow-moving until, about half-way along its course, it plummets abruptly over the spectacular Victoria Falls. Below the falls, the river enters a steep, narrow gorge, plunging and tossing through rapids for more than 250 kilometers (155 miles) before becoming wide and shallow again as it nears the Indian Ocean.

The Zambezi has always been an important habitat for hippos and crocodiles. Elephants, giraffes, zebras, lions, leopards, cheetahs, hyenas, and jackals also come to the river to drink or to hunt.

An African River and a Scottish Doctor

TRADITIONALLY, THE TONGA PEOPLE of Zimbabwe lived along the Zambezi, growing maize (corn) in fields enriched by the river's floods, as well as fishing and hunting along the river's banks. In 1841, a Scottish doctor named David Livingstone arrived in South Africa. Livingstone had come as a medical missionary to "save the souls" of African villagers while helping to improve their health and medical care. But soon he was more interested in traveling through the remote continent than he was in converting people to Christianity or treating illness.

On his journeys, Livingstone witnessed the suffering caused by the African slave trade. Portuguese, Arab, and Swahili slavers were kidnapping men, women, and children from all over Africa. They forced them to march in chains across the country to slave markets on the coasts, where they were sold. From there, many of the slaves were transported across the Atlantic Ocean to work on plantations in the Caribbean islands, Brazil, and the United States.

Livingstone was convinced the only way to stop slavery was to open Africa to other kinds of trade. His motto was: "Christianity, Commerce, and Civilization." But there was no easy way for traders to get to the interior of the continent, and he knew that without a route from the coast, his vision of stopping the slave trade was doomed.

Mapping God's Highway

THEN, WHILE ON A TREK WITH HIS FAMILY, Livingstone encountered the Zambezi River. He realized that if this river, the biggest he had seen in all his travels, was navigable by boat, it could be the route he had been searching for to open up Africa. "God's Highway," he called it, and he was convinced the Zambezi was the answer to ending slavery in Africa: it would be the river of freedom.

For three years, from 1853 to 1856, Livingstone followed the route of the river through Africa. He was sick with malaria most of the time, but he was determined to map the river's course. He was confident that cargo ships would sail up the Zambezi from the Indian Ocean into the heart of Africa, bringing trade and wealth and an end to slavery.

The Queen's Waterfall

IN 1855, LIVINGSTONE'S GUIDES brought him to Mosi-oa-Tunya, the immense waterfall he decided to call Victoria Falls, after Britain's Queen Victoria. When he returned home, he wrote a book describing his river adventures and his "discovery" of the world's largest waterfall. It became an instant best-seller.

The book made Livingstone a celebrity—he was even invited to tea with the queen. But he was only interested in getting back to the Zambezi. Finally, in 1858, the British government agreed to give him a paddle steamer to take up the river. The boat soon ran aground in the shallow water, but Livingstone kept trying—until, only 100 kilometers (62 miles) from the ocean, the steamer met impassable rapids. Livingstone had the boat dismantled and carried piece by piece around the rapids, but the river on the other side was so shallow that they ran aground again and again. The Scottish doctor spent five frustrating years trying to find a route up the Zambezi before the government finally called off the expedition.

THE ST. LAWRENCE: CANADA'S BEAVER HIGHWAY

For thousands of years, the rivers of North America served as highways for aboriginal peoples, who used them for trading and communicating with their neighbors. When the first European explorers arrived, they also used the waterways as the fastest, easiest means of travel across the continent's vast distances.

In the 1500s, French explorers on the St. Lawrence River encountered aboriginal hunters who had been trapping beavers. The explorers took beaver pelts back to Europe, where a fashion craze started for hats made from the soft fur. Soon, beaver pelts were in high demand, and the French and English began setting up trading posts along rivers all across North America, where hunters could exchange pelts for European goods. At the height of the fur trade, so many beavers were trapped that there were far fewer beaver dams on the continent's rivers. Without the dams, the rivers ran faster and carried more sediment, carving new paths and channels and changing their courses. The river highways were changing into super-expressways!

The St. Lawrence River was the key route for transporting furs to Europe, and by the 1700s the fur trade had transformed the village of Montreal into a bustling commercial port. Today, the St. Lawrence remains such an important trade route for Canada, it's known as Highway H_2O.

Scrambling for Africa

LIVINGSTONE'S ZAMBEZI HIGHWAY DREAM was over. However, his book about Africa had captured the imagination of people across Britain and throughout Europe. Until then, the governments of European nations hadn't been interested in Africa; now they realized it was a vast continent filled with riches.

Over the next 25 years, countries including Britain, France, Germany, Belgium, and Portugal moved quickly to gain control of territories in Africa— at the expense of African people, who were mistreated and denied rights to lands they had occupied for generations. Until the mid-20th century, when many African nations began demanding their independence, most African people had no voice in the running of their countries, and they received no share of the profits from Africa's immense natural resources.

It certainly wasn't what Livingstone had hoped for on the day he saw the Zambezi and imagined he had found the route to bring "Christianity, Commerce, and Civilization" to Africa. His exploration of the Zambezi River changed Africa forever, bringing years of misery and turmoil into the lives of people all across the continent.

capetown to cairo:
a BRIDGe over THe ZamBeZI

In 1900, a British businessman decided what Africa needed was a railway—
a massive, continent-spanning route from the tip of South Africa up to Cairo
in the north. The man's name was Cecil Rhodes, and he was rich, powerful,
and ruthless enough to make his vision a reality.

Rhodes owned huge diamond mines in the British colony of South Africa,
and a railroad would get his jewels to markets in Europe more quickly. He
also realized that the railroad's owner could control all of Africa. The British
government agreed, and started construction.

But there was a problem—the Zambezi River was in the way, and there were
no bridges. So Rhodes decided to build a bridge across the river, and the
spot he had in mind was just below Victoria Falls. In a letter to the engineer
he hired to design the bridge, he explained he wanted passengers on his trains
to "catch the spray of the Falls" as they sped past.

Rhodes died while the bridge was being built, and in the end, the Cape to
Cairo Railway was never finished. Britain controlled large parts of Africa at the
time, but so did Germany, Portugal, and France, and they didn't want a British
railroad going through their territories. Construction was often delayed by
wars and uprisings as African people fought to regain control of their lands
from the colonizers. But the bridge over the Zambezi opened in 1905. It's still
used today—and not just for trains. Visitors to Victoria Falls can choose to
bungee jump from the bridge, plummeting 111 meters (364 feet) down toward
the Zambezi, or to fly across the river on a zipline above the falls!

The River Today

Tonga fishers on the Zambezi today paddle dugout canoes not much different from the ones their ancestors used—except for the outboard motors on the back. Using spears, nets, and fish traps, they catch tiger fish, bream, catfish, and bottle fish. They dry their catches at temporary fishing camps—simple reed-walled huts along the river—before taking them to the nearest market town to sell.

Every fisherman knows to keep a watchful eye—and ear—out for hippos, the biggest danger on the river. Hippos will tip over and destroy boats they feel have invaded their territory, and the sounds of snorting and blowing as a hippo's mottled pink head surfaces in the river are the cue to start paddling, hard! Crocodiles are common too, particularly in the man-made lakes behind the two dams across the Zambezi: the Kariba and the Cahora Bassa Dam. Swimming isn't recommended.

There are other hazards along the river: mosquitoes carrying malaria, biting tsetse flies, rapids, and sudden windstorms that can flip a canoe or swamp it. Despite the danger, eco-tourists from around the world come to enjoy the beauty of the Zambezi, floating downstream on rafts or paddling kayaks.

ANGERING THE RIVER GODS

The old people who once lived in traditional Tonga villages along the Zambezi remember the day in 1958 when the "men without knees" came to herd them into trucks and take them to their new homes. The Tonga people, more than 57,000 of them, were being displaced because of a huge dam being built on the Zambezi River: the Kariba Dam. Behind the dam, the river would form a giant lake, flooding the Tonga's traditional homeland.

The men without knees (the Tonga description for white men, who covered their legs with long pants) hastily pushed people onto trucks, some heading for one side of the new lake, others for the opposite shore. Families were split up, separated by hundreds of kilometers of water.

For months, the Tonga leaders had been protesting that damming the river would anger the Zambezi river god, Nyami Nyami. Were they right? Before the dam was even completed, a massive earthquake struck, damaging it badly. For the Tonga, this was a sign from Nyami Nyami.

But the men without knees rebuilt the dam, making it stronger. And although there have been tremors since, Nyami Nyami has not yet destroyed the dam. But the Tonga are confident that one day the dam will fall, and they will be reunited with their families across the water.

7

THAMES

The River That Built an Empire

NAME

The name "Thames" comes from the Celtic word *tamesas*, meaning "dark." By the time it reaches London, the Thames River has a high silt content, turning it a deep brown color.

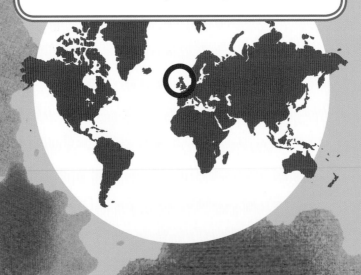

LENGTH
346 km
(215 miles)

HEADWATERS
Thames Head, a small spring near the town of Cirencester in the Cotswold Hills, west of London

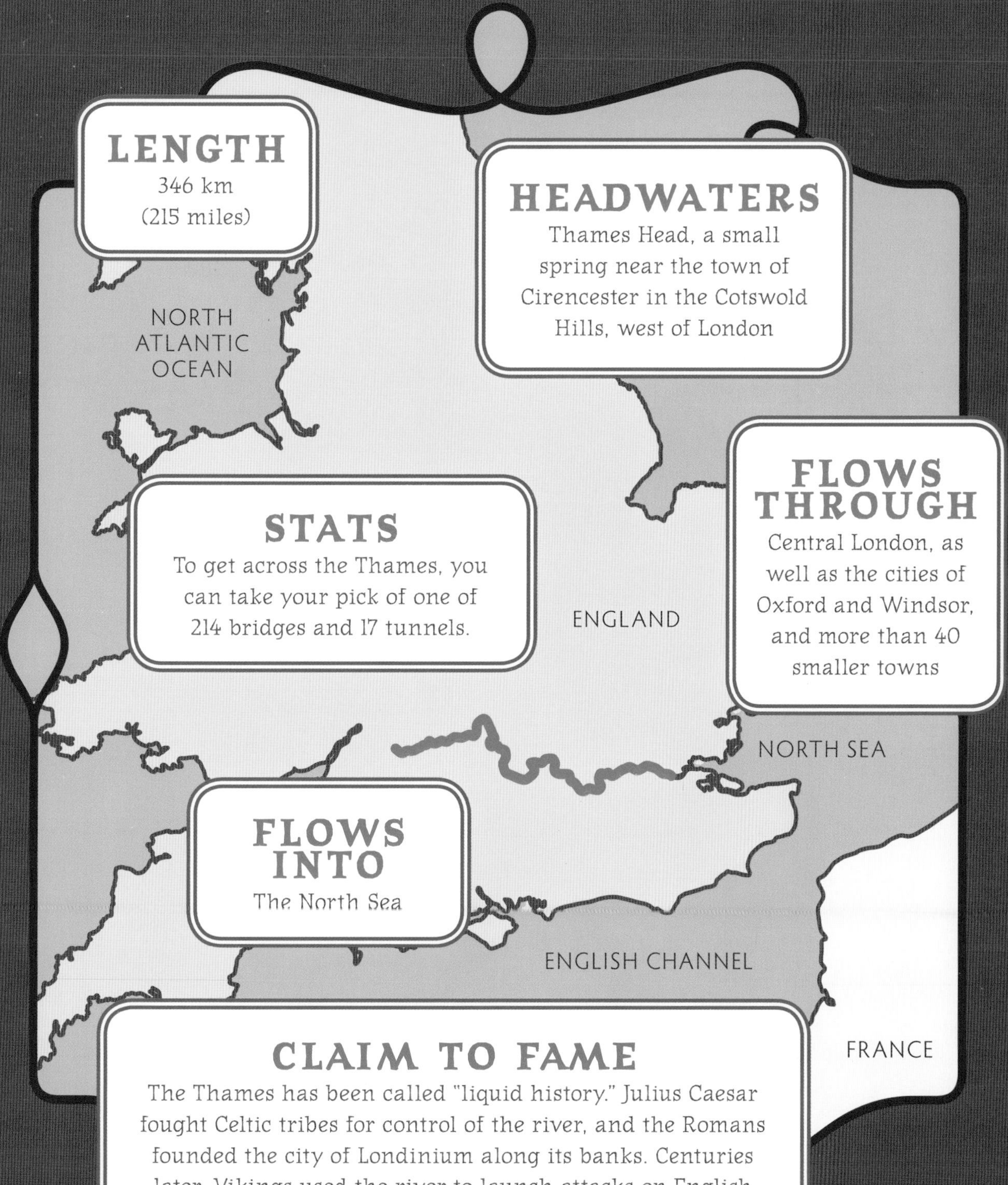

NORTH ATLANTIC OCEAN

FLOWS THROUGH
Central London, as well as the cities of Oxford and Windsor, and more than 40 smaller towns

STATS
To get across the Thames, you can take your pick of one of 214 bridges and 17 tunnels.

ENGLAND

NORTH SEA

FLOWS INTO
The North Sea

ENGLISH CHANNEL

FRANCE

CLAIM TO FAME
The Thames has been called "liquid history." Julius Caesar fought Celtic tribes for control of the river, and the Romans founded the city of Londinium along its banks. Centuries later, Vikings used the river to launch attacks on English cities. Starting in the 16th century, docks for oceangoing ships along the Thames turned London into a worldwide center for trade, making it the heart of the British Empire.

LONDON
[1824]

The night sky was just beginning to lighten, and James and Lizzie had already been up for almost an hour. Lizzie was shivering—her dress was thin, and she had no shoes. Nevertheless, she hurried to keep up with her big brother.

"How do we get down to the river, James?" Lizzie asked.

"Stairs," he answered. "We'll try the Horseshoe Alley stairs. If there's too many others there, we'll move over to the Old Swan stairs, or Pepper Alley stairs right under London Bridge. It can be good picking there, but sometimes there's things you'd rather not see beneath the bridge. Things folks have tossed over."

He didn't explain, and Lizzie was too nervous to ask more questions. Just the night before, her mother had told her it was time for her to start working—scavenging with her brother along the Thames. "You're six now, Lizzie. You're big and strong, and you know we need the money," her mother had said encouragingly. "Do as James tells you, use your eyes, and you'll soon catch on."

At the bottom of the long stone flight of steps, Lizzie gasped in surprise. In the streets above, London was still sleeping, but down here the workday had begun. On the river, boatmen were pulling hard at their oars, transferring loads from the ships anchored in the channel to the waiting workers on the docks. Others were ferrying passengers back and forth across the river. The tide was out, exposing wide muddy flats, and men in long, flapping coats paced the ground, probing ahead of them with poles to test for firmness. Herds of ragged children followed them, jostling and scrabbling in the wet dirt.

"Toshers," said James, pointing to the men with poles. "They get the good stuff—coins, metal, sometimes even jewels. What they leave behind, that's what us mudlarks can take. Coal's the best. But if you see a bit of wood, or a piece of cloth or rope, pick it up. Anything we find we'll try to sell."

They stepped out onto the river flats, sinking up to their ankles in cold mud. James bent down, and with a grunt, tugged up a wet black rock. "Coal, first try! Here, Lizzie, you take it." Gagging at the smell of the foul mud, Lizzie grabbed the dripping lump and shoved it in her pocket. She was a mudlark now.

The Story of the Thames

Although it has a long history, the Thames is actually a
short river. It starts as a quiet stream in the green English countryside,
winds through little villages and past the ancient stone halls of Oxford
University, then arrives in London. There, it sweeps grandly under
the Tower Bridge and past famous landmarks like Big Ben, the Tower
of London, St. Paul's Cathedral, and the Palace of Westminster, before
making its way south to the sea.

Where the river meets the sea in the Thames Estuary, and occasionally swimming upstream as far as London, a number of exotic visitors
are found, including seals, dolphins, porpoises, and even sea horses.
When a pod of porpoises was spotted in 2013 frolicking in the river
in the middle of London, it made international news. But the Thames

is also known for its native wildlife—the moles, toads, water rats, badgers, and otters that live in the water meadows and woods along the upper reaches of the river.

In 1908 a writer named Kenneth Grahame published a children's book set along the river, called *The Wind in the Willows*. It described the adventures of a little band of animals "messing about in boats" on the river. His book made the Thames famous in a new way, as a gentle country stream rather than one of the world's major shipping routes. Today, while many visitors to Britain only see the Thames as it flows through London, you can also follow a meandering riverside trail through the English countryside, all the way from its source to the sea.

JELLIED EEL, ANYONE?

Eels are among the oddest inhabitants of the Thames. They arrive in the river as tiny larvae, after journeying over 6,000 kilometers (3,700 miles) from an area of the Atlantic Ocean known as the Sargasso Sea. The eels stay in the Thames for 20 years before making the long trip back home to spawn.

In the 1700s, pubs and street stalls in the poorer areas of London began selling a dish called jellied eels. The recipe was simple: chopped eels, boiled with herbs until soft. When the dish cooled, it formed a jellied mass, because eels contain natural gelatin. Unlikely as it sounds, jellied eels caught on. They're still popular, sold in restaurants and supermarkets all around Britain.

London Bridge Is Falling Down...

THE OLD CHILDREN'S NURSERY RHYME may have its roots
in history. In 1014, a party of Vikings sailed up the Thames to loot
London. When they couldn't get past a wooden bridge in the river
at the entrance to the city, they simply tied ropes to the piers of the
bridge, waited for the tide to turn, and sailed off downstream, pulling
the bridge down behind them. Then they returned to pillage the city!

Soon afterward, Londoners decided they needed a stronger bridge
to keep the Vikings out. People got to work, and 30 years later, London
Bridge was finished—a massive construction with 19 stone arches over
the river. The bridge had been so expensive to build that the city
decided to rent out space on it. Soon shops, houses, and even churches
appeared on London Bridge, and it was on its way to becoming one
of the wonders of medieval Europe. For the next five centuries the
crowded bridge stood guard over the city.

Trading with the World

It wasn't just Viking boats that were stopped by London Bridge—so were ships carrying goods and cargo to English cities upstream. They had to unload their freight at the river docks in London, and that kept the port busy and made London rich. As early as the 12th century, ships from Arabia, Egypt, Russia, France, Turkey, and Venice were bringing precious cargoes up the Thames to London. Pepper, tobacco, tea, cinnamon, sugar, rum, silk, and gold all made their way up the river.

To service these ships, wharves and jetties and docks were built, along with warehouses, stores, taverns, inns, and houses for sailors and river workers. Shipbuilding yards sprang up, and so did mills and factories of all kinds—glassmakers, paint and dye manufacturers, sugar refineries, leather tanneries, and breweries. London became a world center of trade, and as England established its empire, the colonies in India, North and South America, Africa, and Asia sent their treasures by ship to the docks along the Thames.

WORKING THE RIVER

During the 18th and 19th centuries, more than 40,000 people earned their living from the Thames. The river was so crowded with ships it was said you could walk from shore to shore across all the boats and barges. Here are some of the jobs you could have held:

LIGHTERMEN rowed wide, flat-bottomed barges called lighters, which were used to unload (or lighten) merchant ships anchored in the Thames, bringing their cargo to the docks in the Port of London.

LUMPERS loaded the cargo from seagoing ships onto the lighters.

WATERMEN ferried passengers across the river in small open boats called wherries or skiffs. One man rowed the boat, while an apprentice helped passengers on and off, and collected their fares.

DOCKERS (also called stevedores) unloaded the cargo and carried it into the warehouses lining the river.

FLUSHERMEN worked in the covered rivers flowing into the Thames that acted as the city's sewers, making sure they didn't become blocked.

PURLMEN sold beer to river workers from small boats.

There were also those who made a living from the river in less legitimate ways:

SCUFFLE HUNTERS stole goods from the docks.

HEAVY HORSEMEN were porters and laborers who hid stolen goods in their baggy clothes.

NIGHT PLUNDERERS cut barges loose and then looted them downstream.

What a Waste!

As the Thames got busier and industry increased, the river got dirtier. It was the place to dump anything unwanted: garbage, dead animals, rotten food, and human waste. People hoped everything would get carried out to sea. But the filth was just as likely to get pushed back up the river by the incoming tide. The river became a sludge of garbage and poisons.

The problem just got worse the bigger London grew. Then something happened that prompted a river crisis. In 1851, the first working flush toilet was unveiled at the Great Exhibition in London. It was one of the biggest attractions at the fair. Nearly a million fairgoers lined up to use it and soon everyone wanted one installed in their home. Within a few years, over 200,000 homes in London had flush toilets connected to sewers.

But what Londoners thought they were flushing away was actually running straight into the Thames. And so the river got smellier and smellier.

The Great Exhibition of 1851

FROSTY RIVER FUN

Lightermen, toshers, watermen, and dockers—they all depended on the river to earn their living. So what did they do when it froze over?

Between 1684 and 1814, there were 23 years when the Thames froze solid. And when it happened, the out-of-work river laborers put on a fair, hoping to bring wealthy Londoners down to the river for a massive party. There were booths selling gingerbread, hot cider, and beer. Plays were performed, using barges frozen into the ice as stages. In 1814, an elephant was paraded across the frozen river. And printers brought their printing presses down to the ice to create instant souvenirs. One 1814 souvenir pamphlet read: "Whereas you, J Frost, have by force and violence taken possession of the river THAMES, I hereby give you warning to quit immediately. Signed, A Thaw." That was the last year the Thames froze hard enough for a frost fair. The warning must have worked!

That Stinks!

The summer of 1858 was long, hot, and dry. In London, there was no rain for weeks, and as the water level in the Thames dropped, the contents of the river were exposed. The terrible smell spread throughout the city. Newspapers called it "the Great Stink," and anyone who could afford it left London that summer. Even parliament was suspended. When the members of parliament got back to work in the fall, they agreed it was time to clean up the river.

Joseph Bazalgette, the city's chief sanitary engineer, proposed a plan to build a massive system of sewers that would carry all London's waste far down the river, away from the city. For the system to work, his team of men would have to dig 1,930 kilometers (1,200 miles) of tunnels underneath the busy city streets. That's more than five times the whole length of the Thames River!

It took 10 years, used 318 million bricks (to line all those miles of tunnels), and cost 3 million pounds, but the sewage system Bazalgette designed and built is still in use today. Cities across the world quickly followed London's example and installed sewer systems to protect the health of their citizens and clean up dirty rivers.

THE RIVER AT WAR

Night after night during the Second World War, bombs dropped by German planes exploded across London. To protect the city, London was placed under a strict blackout order: streetlights were shut off and people kept their curtains tightly closed so that no light would escape to guide the enemy planes. Yet every night the bombs found their targets. German pilots simply followed the Thames River upstream from the coast. The east end of the city was the hardest hit, because it was closest to the docks and shipyards along the river.

THE TONE RIVER: NATURAL OR MAN-MADE?

Like London, Tokyo is one of the world's largest, most important cities. But in the 1600s, Tokyo was just a small town (then known as Edo, which means "entrance to the bay" or "estuary") on the banks of the Tone River. The river made life in Edo tough. Terrible floods swamped the city, damaging buildings and killing people.

Edo's leaders decided to take action before the river destroyed the city. In other parts of the world, cities had been abandoned once river floods got out of control, but the Japanese shogun (a military commander) had just built a magnificent and expensive castle at Edo. So instead of moving the city, the leaders hatched a plan to move the river.

It took more than 50 years, but at last they succeeded. Thanks to thousands of laborers, they diverted the Tone River 100 kilometers (62 miles) to the east. That was close enough that goods could still be shipped easily to and from the city, but far enough away to keep everyone safe and dry. By 1720, Edo was Japan's largest city, with a population of about 1.4 million. It's kept on growing: today, the city we now know as Tokyo is home to over 13 million people.

Mudlarks Today

Today, the Thames is cleaner than it has been for centuries. But mudlarks are still hunting along the shores for things people have thrown away. Today's mudlarks aren't ragged children; they're adults with metal detectors, and they're looking for treasure, because the Thames riverbank is one of the world's biggest archaeological sites. Chain mail, Roman coins, ancient jewelry—it's all there in the mud of the Thames.

These mudlarks don't sell what they dig out of the riverbanks—they turn their discoveries over to the Museum of London. In the past 30 years, the museum has collected 90,000 artifacts this way! And each piece helps to tell the story of how Londoners have lived with and used the river over many centuries.

The thick, sulphur-smelling mud of the Thames has very little oxygen in it, so anything trapped in the mud is perfectly preserved. Out of the mud, mudlarks have pulled leather shoes worn by ancient Romans, toys lost by children in the Middle Ages, and daggers that may have dropped overboard during shipboard fights centuries ago.

MISSISSIPPI

River of Song

NAME

The name "Mississippi" comes from the Ojibwe language: *Misi-ziibi*, or "great river." It is also known as Old Man River, Ole Muddy, Father of Waters, and Ole Glory.

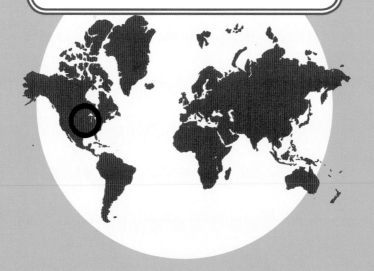

CANADA

HEADWATERS
Lake Itasca, in northern Minnesota

WISCONSIN

MINNESOTA

IOWA

FLOWS THROUGH
Minnesota, Wisconsin, Illinois, Iowa, Missouri, Kentucky, Tennessee, Arkansas, Mississippi, Louisiana

LENGTH
3,780 km
(2,349 miles)

ILLINOIS

MISSOURI

KENTUCKY

ARKANSAS

TENNESSEE

FLOWS INTO
The Gulf of Mexico, at New Orleans

LOUISIANA

MISSISSIPPI

GULF OF MEXICO

STATS
It takes 90 days for a drop of water to travel the length of the Mississippi River.

CLAIM TO FAME
In the early part of the 20th century, the Mississippi was a musical highway. Jazz, blues, and rock and roll all got their start in the Mississippi Delta, traveling up the river with musicians making their way from New Orleans to the big cities of the north.

NEW ORLEANS, LOUISIANA
[1921]

With his horn tucked under his arm and his small suitcase swinging from his hand, Louis Armstrong raced down the crowded streets of New Orleans. He was late.

In just a few minutes, the SS Sidney would pull away from the docks and start steaming its way up the Mississippi River. The ship wouldn't be back in New Orleans for months. And if Louis didn't make it before the Sidney left, he'd be out of a job.

Louis had been blowing his trumpet in a street-corner band, playing for spare change outside a New Orleans dance hall when Fate Marable, the legendary bandleader, stopped by to listen. Fate offered the young trumpeter a spot in his riverboat jazz band, playing every night all summer long in towns along the Mississippi.

It was a great opportunity—he'd play with professional musicians, in front of bigger audiences than he'd ever dreamt of, and he'd see the world. Seventeen-year-old Louis had never been out of New Orleans before. If he could just get to the Sidney in time …

Suddenly, there it was, floating on the muddy waves, a massive white wedding cake of a ship. Louis's eyes widened as he gazed up at the decks draped in colorful bunting, the hundreds of twinkling white lights, and the immense red and white paddle wheel at the stern.

Onboard, the band members, dressed in identical white suits, were already warming up. Louis found a spot behind the pianist and put his trumpet to his lips. Soon, the dance floor was crowded with couples swinging to the music. Louis stood up and started a long, wild horn solo that got the audience cheering and clapping. "Go, man, go!" yelled Fate. As Louis ended his solo, he knew it was going to be a good summer.

A flooded pavilion in Minnesota

The Story of the Mississippi

THE MISSISSIPPI HAS ALWAYS HAD A REPUTATION as a treacherous river, full of hidden sandbars and snags where boats run aground, whirlpools that can catch a small boat and suck it under, and wide pools in which the current disappears and boats can become trapped. It is known for its epic floods, and for constantly changing its course, carving new channels and leaving the old ones abandoned and dry. The U.S. Army has a special Corps of Engineers whose job is to tame the Mississippi, by straightening its banks and building locks to keep water levels steady, but the river keeps breaking out in new ways, resisting human attempts to control it.

The mighty Mississippi runs south from Minnesota's Lake Itasca, near the Canadian border, all the way down to the Gulf of Mexico.

Before the arrival of Europeans, the lands along the river were home to the Mississippian culture, Native Americans who built large cities and towns, grew corn in the flat, fertile lands along the river, and traveled its waters to trade and wage war with other tribes. In the north, the Sioux, Ojibwe, Pottawatomie, Illini, Menominee, and Winnebago peoples lived along the river, while further south were the Choctaw, Chickasaw, Quapaw, Osage, Caddo, and Natchez. In 1541, the Spanish conquistador Hernando de Soto became the first European to see the Mississippi River and to visit the cities of the Mississippian peoples.

Over the next few centuries, as more and more Europeans came to North America, some brave pioneers ventured onto the Mississippi, traveling the mighty river in boats and rafts, settling along its banks—and displacing the Native people. Many Mississippians abandoned their villages and headed west, away from the new settlers. Along the southern Mississippi, cotton plantations worked by African slaves took the place of Native American cities.

African-Americans had a long history of working on the Mississippi well before musicians like Louis Armstrong began playing riverboat jazz. For former slaves in the American South, working on the river was one of the few jobs that gave them the opportunity to travel. "Free blacks" worked as deckhands, sailors, cooks, and porters on ships traveling up and down the river, and as night watchmen and roustabouts on the docks and warehouses lining the riverbanks.

Music of the Mississippi

IF IT WEREN'T FOR THE MISSISSIPPI RIVER, we'd all probably listen to a lot more opera. Or Balinese gamelan music. Or maybe Spanish flamenco. That's because almost all of today's popular music, including rock, country, and hip-hop, has roots in the jazz and blues of the Mississippi Delta.

In the late 1800s, black laborers—many of them newly freed slaves—were clearing the Mississippi Delta for farms. People have probably

THE ADVENTURES OF
HUCKLEBERRY FINN

USA 29

LIFE ON THE MISSISSIPPI

Mark Twain's famous book *The Adventures of Huckleberry Finn* (1884) changed literature around the world. It's the story of Huck Finn and his friend Jim, a runaway slave, rafting down the Mississippi. What made the book different was the colorful way the characters spoke: they used slang and made grammatical mistakes. In fact, they sounded just like regular country folks—something no writer had ever tried before. Some readers were shocked, but most loved the book. It's become one of the classic stories of all time—thanks to Mark Twain's knowledge of the life along the river.

Twain grew up playing on the river in Hannibal, Missouri. Of course, he wasn't Mark Twain then—Samuel Clemens was the name he was born with. As an adult, Samuel got his dream job, becoming a Mississippi riverboat pilot. But when the American Civil War broke out, the Mississippi wasn't safe any longer, so Samuel headed west, working as a newspaper reporter. He decided to publish some of his more outrageous articles under a different name: "Mark Twain"—a Mississippi riverboat term for water at least two fathoms (about 3.7 meters, or 12 feet) deep, enough to allow riverboats through.

always sung while they worked, but as these workers sang, a unique new musical style developed. Their music wasn't just a way to make the work easier, it was also a way to express how they felt—often sad and frustrated, yet hopeful too. The songs combined rhythms and words from Christian hymns, African chants, and traditional work songs. That blend became what is today called the Delta blues.

Meanwhile, a little farther upriver in St. Louis, Missouri, a style of music called ragtime was becoming popular. Ragtime was dance music with a wild beat, and an African-American musician called Scott Joplin became known as the King of Ragtime.

Storyville Stylings: The Birth of Jazz

AT THE BEGINNING OF THE 20TH CENTURY, the biggest city was New Orleans. It was one of the world's busiest ports, and people from all over the globe met and mingled in the riverside bars and dance halls of a neighborhood called Storyville. The Storyville musicians blended Delta blues and ragtime with influences from around the world. They also did their best to make their small bands sound like big orchestras, which meant the players all became experts at improvising and getting different sounds out of their instruments. Audiences loved the unpredictability of the new style, and soon jazz was born.

Then, in 1917, the New Orleans city government decided to clean up the riverside. They closed down Storyville's ramshackle dance halls, and musicians had to look elsewhere for places to play. At the same time, riverboat operators were searching for a new way to make money. Moving the dance halls onto the boats was the perfect solution, and soon New Orleans musicians were taking their sounds up the river. As one song put it: "Jazz came up the river from New Orleans / Looking for a better-paying job it seems."

The new hot jazz music also traveled overland to Chicago and New York, and from there to Europe and across the globe.

captain Blanche Leathers

Born on a Mississippi cotton plantation, young Blanche had always loved the river. When she grew up and married a steamboat captain, she insisted on traveling the Mississippi at his side. Soon she learned to read the river, to recognize every bend and understand the meaning of every ripple. She could navigate its dangerous channels on even the blackest of moonless nights, or in the thickest fogs. Eventually, Blanche Leathers decided to apply for a captain's license of her own.

It was a daring move for a woman in the 1880s, when the Mississippi was still a man's world. But Blanche passed the captain's test and was given the command of a Mississippi steamboat. When she steamed out of New Orleans at the helm of the *Natchez* on her maiden voyage, every vessel in the harbor saluted her with a blast of its whistle. For more than 20 years, Captain Blanche navigated up and down the Mississippi, carrying cotton, riverboat gamblers, even a U.S. president. She helped to change life for women in the American South as well, by proving a woman could succeed at a dangerous job.

Louis Armstrong, the Luckiest Horn Player

LOUIS ARMSTRONG DIDN'T HAVE A GREAT START IN LIFE. He was born in the slums of New Orleans, and his family was so poor he couldn't go to school. Instead, he hung around the streets, looking for food or work and getting into trouble. When he was 10, he was arrested for shooting off his mother's gun on New Year's Eve, and sent to a local reform school, the Waifs' Home for Boys.

It may have been the luckiest thing that ever happened to him. The Waifs' Home had a brass band, and soon Louis was desperate to join. He talked the bandleader into teaching him to play the trumpet, and suddenly the future for young Louis looked much different. It turned out Louis had a great musical gift, and his outgoing personality made him a huge hit with audiences. By the 1940s, Louis Armstrong was one of the most famous entertainers on the planet.

Louis Armstrong changed musical history, making jazz the most popular musical style of the day. He recorded thousands of songs, and some of them, like "Hello Dolly," "Mack the Knife," "Up the Lazy River," and "What a Wonderful World," are still played today.

The Story Continues

In the 1950s, another town along the Mississippi became a musical hotbed: Memphis, Tennessee. Young performers like Elvis Presley and Jerry Lee Lewis blended the sounds of blues music with the rhythms of guitar and drums, creating a new style of music they called "rock 'n' roll." Once more, the world would never be the same.

Today, riverboats still travel up and down the Mississippi playing jazz and blues for tourists who want to relive the magic and romance of the river's past.

Statue of Johann Strauss in Vienna, Austria

THE DANUBE RIVER: MORE RIVER BLUES?

You'll know it's midnight on New Year's Eve in Austria when the radio starts to play "The Blue Danube," a waltz by Johann Strauss. It's an annual tradition in Austria, where "The Blue Danube" has been adopted as a kind of unofficial national anthem. The song has been loved by music fans for nearly 150 years, and no one seems to mind—or notice—that the Danube River isn't actually blue (it's a muddy yellow-green).

Although it's now one of the best-known pieces of classical music in the world, "The Blue Danube" flopped the first time it was played, in Vienna in 1858. "The devil take my waltz," Strauss complained after the performance. He'd be encouraged to know that today the Danube River is so closely associated with classical music that special cruise ships tour the river, bringing travelers to explore the musical history of the cities along the banks and their celebrated composers, including Strauss himself, Mozart, Beethoven, and Chopin. And as weary residents complain, more often than not, the ships' loudspeakers are playing ... "The Blue Danube" waltz.

9

GANGES

River of Faith

NAME
"Ganges" comes from the Sanskrit word *ganga*, meaning "swift-goer." In India, the Ganges is also known by no fewer than 108 other names. One of the most common is *Ganga Ma*, or Mother Ganges.

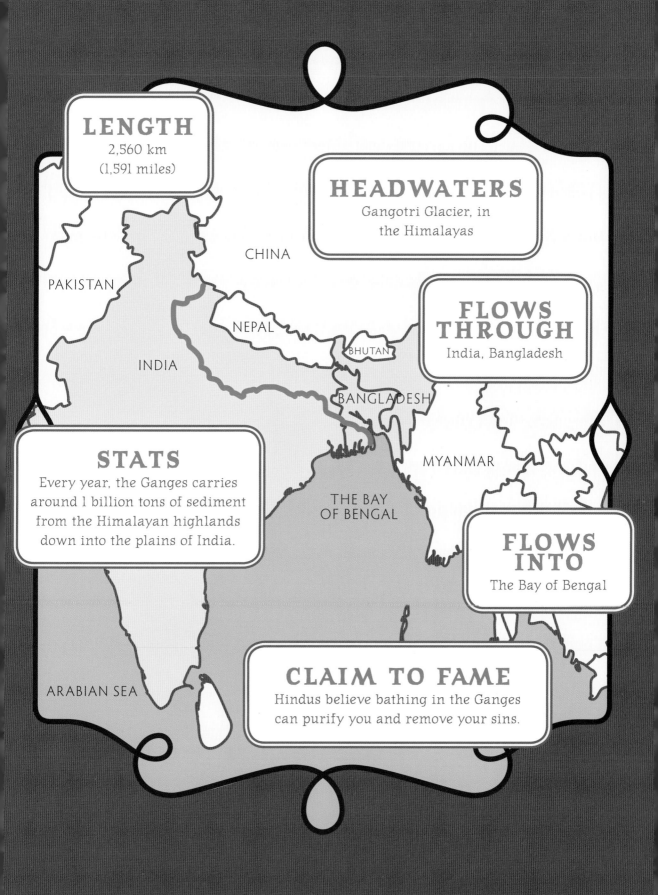

LENGTH
2,560 km
(1,591 miles)

HEADWATERS
Gangotri Glacier, in
the Himalayas

FLOWS THROUGH
India, Bangladesh

STATS
Every year, the Ganges carries
around 1 billion tons of sediment
from the Himalayan highlands
down into the plains of India.

FLOWS INTO
The Bay of Bengal

CLAIM TO FAME
Hindus believe bathing in the Ganges
can purify you and remove your sins.

CHINA

PAKISTAN

NEPAL

BHUTAN

INDIA

BANGLADESH

MYANMAR

THE BAY
OF BENGAL

ARABIAN SEA

ALLAHABAD
[JANUARY 2013]

As his father's car bumped up onto the bridge over the Ganges, Sunil stared out the window. Across the river lay the city of Allahabad, but beneath them on the riverbank lay another city—a sprawling tent city. As far as Sunil's eyes could see, lines of tents stretched away on the white sand of the riverbed and far, far up the banks. He turned to look in the other direction, and the same sight met his eyes: a sea of tents—some tiny, some as big as circus tents and lit with twinkling lights.

"How will we find our tent, Dad?" Sunil never imagined the Kumbh Mela festival would be so enormous.

"I've got the address right here: Santoshi Marg, along from Pontoon Bridge number 8. Every tent has its own address, Sunil—don't worry. But first let's visit the river."

Leaving their car parked in a vast crowded field, they wove on foot through the crowds of pilgrims with freshly shaved heads, and among the groups of chanting sadhus (holy men)—some striped and daubed with ash, some naked and holding long spears. They walked along the rows of traders—the bangle sellers, water stalls, barbers, bookshops, tea stalls, bead vendors, incense sellers—until at last they reached the edge of the Ganges.

Golden light from the setting sun glinted on the surface of the water, silhouetting the hundreds of bathers standing waist-deep in the river. Sunil and his father waded in among them, plunging their hands into the cold water and then raising them, dripping, to the sun. Music blasted from speakers, banners flapped, and all around them bathers chanted, "Jai Ganga Maiya"—"Long live Mother Ganga." Sunil splashed himself, thinking, "I am here too, holy Mother Ganges. I have come to worship you."

The Story of the Ganges

THE SOURCE OF THE GANGES is an ice cave high in the
Himalayan mountains, near India's border with Tibet. Melting
water from the Gangotri Glacier flows out of the ice cave and forms
a small stream called the Bhagirathi River. For 200 kilometers
(124 miles), the Bhagirathi churns through high mountain valleys,
until it meets the Alaknanda River. At the confluence (the joining
of two rivers), the river becomes known as the Ganges.

Farther along its course, at the city of Allahabad, the Yamuna
River joins the Ganges. It continues flowing southeast, past the
holy city of Varanasi, before emptying into the Bay of Bengal, in
Bangladesh.

River of Faith

HINDUS HAVE WORSHIPPED THE GANGES as a sacred river for more than 3,500 years. They believe that the water of the Ganges has very special powers: it can heal the body, grant wishes, even send your soul to paradise.

For that reason, it's considered a good place to die. If your body is cremated along the shores of the Ganges, Hindus say, and the ashes are sprinkled in the water, you will go immediately to paradise. The city of Varanasi specializes in cremations: on broad steps along the riverbanks at the city's many cremation areas, up to 80 bodies are burned each day.

WEARING DOWN THE MOUNTAINS

Until the 1700s, the Ganges was deep enough for large boats to sail up the river as far as Allahabad. Since then, the river has become so clogged with sediment that only very shallow boats can navigate it.

All the sediment the Ganges carries downstream from the Himalayas every year is deposited in the flat Ganges Delta in Bangladesh, where the river flows into the Bay of Bengal. There it forms the sandbanks and islands of the Sundarbans, the largest coastal forest on earth, which helps to prevent seawater from flooding inland during high tides and tropical storms. That protection is important for low-lying Bangladesh. Even so, up to 40 percent of the country is flooded during monsoon season every year.

The World's Biggest Party

Every 12 years, millions of pilgrims from all over India and around the world come together at the city of Allahabad for the Kumbh Mela. Allahabad is a holy spot for Hindus. The Ganges and the Yamuna rivers join here, and according to Hindu tradition, a third river flows into them as well: the Sarasvati, a mythical underground stream invisible to the human eye. During the Kumbh Mela, for 55 days in January and February, pilgrims celebrate and worship the rivers, bathing in the water and making offerings. Flowers, fruit, and sweets are given to the river, sent bobbing away on tiny clay boats lit with candles.

The first mela (it means "fair" in Sanskrit) was held in the seventh century CE, although it's likely been celebrated for much longer. In 2013, 100 million people attended the Kumbh Mela, making it the largest gathering in history.

LIFE ALONG THE RIVER

As well as being a sacred river, the Ganges is a working river. Millions of people depend on it for their livelihood—among them India's traditional washermen, the dhobi wallahs. Each morning, dhobi wallahs collect bundles of soiled laundry from their customers, taking them down to the dhobi ghats: wide stone steps leading into the river. They soak the clothes in the river, beating the dirt out on rocks or on the steps, before spreading the laundry to dry in the afternoon sun.

At the end of the day, the dhobi wallah collects, irons, and folds the clean, dry clothes, carefully returning each shirt, towel, and sari (the traditional long draped garment worn by Indian women) to its proper owner. It's a system that has worked for centuries.

Get Organized!

ORGANIZING A FESTIVAL FOR MILLIONS OF PEOPLE is a lot of work. Where will they all sleep? Where will they eat, and what will they eat? The state government starts planning years in advance for each Kumbh Mela. They build massive campgrounds along the riverbanks, with thousands of tents in orderly rows. Every temporary street has a name, and every tent has an address, so people can find their way. Electricity, safe drinking water, washrooms, cooking facilities, and even a special police force are set up for the tent city.

But when hundreds of thousands of bathers crowd into the river at the same time, people often get separated. At the 2001 Kumbh Mela, 20,000 people got lost each day. While cell phones helped some find their way back to their families, most people relied on announcements made over loudspeakers, and on good luck.

Drinking the Water of Immortality

HINDUS BELIEVE THE WATER OF THE GANGES RIVER has special purifying powers. In the 16th century, the Indian emperor Akbar called it the "water of immortality" and made sure he always had a supply with him when he traveled. In the 19th century, British traders taking goods back from India believed in the power of Ganges water too: before a ship sailed for the three-month journey to England, it would always take water from the river along for passengers to drink. Ships' captains reported that only Ganges water stayed "sweet and fresh" for the entire trip.

Today, the Ganges is under threat from pollution—from industry, from pesticides that run off fields into the river, and from the untreated sewage that gets pumped directly into the water by towns and cities along its banks.

Many people in India are working to clean up the river, but others say it isn't necessary. They argue the Ganges has special properties that help to cleanse the water. Some believe the water of the Ganges contains more oxygen than other rivers do, or has more bacteriophages (viruses that destroy bacteria), which could explain why people don't get sick more often from drinking it and bathing in it. So far, however, none of these claims have been proven. If Ganges water really does have special powers, we still don't know what they are.

THE JORDAN: HOLY RIVERS!

The rushing waters of rivers symbolize purity to people of many religious faiths, and there are rivers all over the world that are believed to be home to gods. One famous holy river is the Jordan River, which runs through the countries of Israel and Jordan to the Dead Sea. For at least 2,000 years, Christians, Jews, and Muslims have considered the Jordan River sacred, and they believe that many miracles happened in it or near it.

For Christians, the Jordan River is most important as the place where Jesus was baptized. A baptism is a religious ritual that symbolizes a person has been "reborn" into a new life, and it always involves water. Some people may be baptized with just a sprinkle of water on their foreheads, but others—as Jesus did—choose to plunge themselves right into a river.

To slaves in the American South in the 1800s, the River Jordan also symbolized freedom. Slaves sang songs like "Swing Low, Sweet Chariot," which includes the lyrics, "I looked over Jordan and what did I see/ Coming for to carry me home? A band of angels coming after me." Many music historians think those lyrics were a kind of code slaves used to express their hopes of escaping to freedom through the Underground Railroad, a network of secret routes to the northern states and Canada.

10

YANGTZE

A Changing River

NAME

The Yangtze is also known as *Chang Jiang* ("Long River"), *Jinsha Jiang* ("River of Golden Sand"), and *Tongtian He* ("River to Heaven").

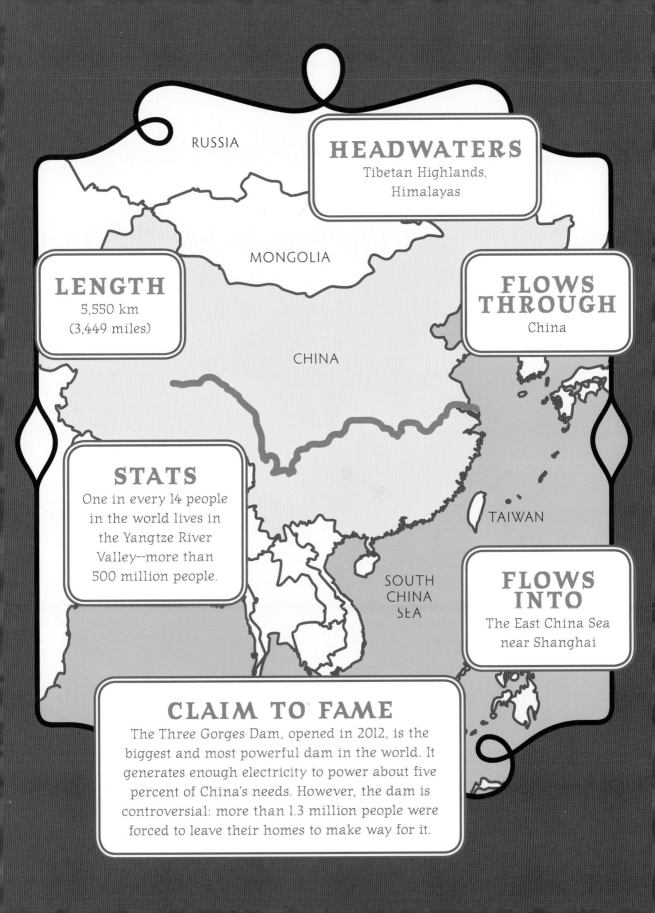

HEADWATERS
Tibetan Highlands, Himalayas

RUSSIA

MONGOLIA

LENGTH
5,550 km
(3,449 miles)

FLOWS THROUGH
China

CHINA

STATS
One in every 14 people in the world lives in the Yangtze River Valley—more than 500 million people.

TAIWAN

FLOWS INTO
The East China Sea near Shanghai

SOUTH CHINA SEA

CLAIM TO FAME
The Three Gorges Dam, opened in 2012, is the biggest and most powerful dam in the world. It generates enough electricity to power about five percent of China's needs. However, the dam is controversial: more than 1.3 million people were forced to leave their homes to make way for it.

HANKOU
[1911]

"Watch out, coming through! Excuse me, important business, please move aside." On Hankou's crowded dockside, you needed either a big voice or a lot of self-confidence to push your way through to the ships. Li Pang was lucky—he had both. His boss, a rich tea merchant, had sent young Li down to the river to oversee the loading of the company's junks. And Li Pang knew better than to be late: if a single chest of tea went missing, his wages would be docked.

He pushed and bustled and shouted through the dark, narrow lanes, edging past sweating coolies pulling loads, bowing low as a mandarin was carried past in his gilded chair, ducking under the swinging red and gold signboards of the tiny shops. When the sweet smell of incense gave way to a fresh river breeze, he knew he was getting close.

Once on the docks, he had to find the right ship—no easy matter since the brightly colored junks were crowded three or four deep all along the riverside, and their cargoes were piled up everywhere. Bales of raw silk, crates of rice, sacks of lotus root, vats of sesame oil, bean curd, and tung oil. And tea: towering stacks of boxes, bags, and chests full of jasmine tea, oolong tea, and the famous gunpowder tea, all ready to send to foreign lands. Li Pang spotted his master's junk and began edging his way over.

But before he could get to the ship, a tall figure blocked his way. "Move, please," Li Pang shouted impatiently. When the man turned around, Li Pang gasped. It was Sun Yat-sen, the man the newspapers had promised would return any day from abroad to lead the country and overthrow the corrupt imperial government. The famous man smiled at Li Pang. "You, with the big voice. Help me find the ship that's supposed to take me up the river to Nanjing. In this crowd, I've lost my bearings."

"Yes, sir!" Bursting with pride, Li Pang rushed ahead, ready to knock anyone who got in his way into the Yangtze. Change was coming to China, and he was a part of it!

The Story of the Yangtze

From its source in the Tibetan highlands, China's Yangtze River flows south for well over 1,000 kilometers (620 miles). Then it changes its mind. Near a town called Shigu in the western province of Yunnan, the river twists into an S shape and starts to flow east across China, finally emptying into the sea near the city of Shanghai.

Because it crosses almost the entire country, the Yangtze is considered the most important river in China. But what if it hadn't made that turn? What if instead it had continued south, leaving China and entering Vietnam? Then the Yangtze wouldn't be China's great river at all, and thousands of kilometers of fertile land in the heart of the country might be a desert.

Geologists point out that at Shigu, the Yangtze River runs into impenetrable limestone cliffs. Unable to carve a channel through the hard rock, the water is forced around the cliffs, which alters the river's course. But according to Chinese legends, there is another explanation. According to the stories, 4,000 years ago, Emperor Da Yu (known as Yu the Great) saw the Yangtze trying to escape from China. To stop it he put a mountain in the river's path at Shigu. Da Yu's mountain, called Yunling, or "cloud mountain," kept the Yangtze in China, changing the country's history forever.

Other emperors haven't been as successful as Da Yu at controlling the Yangtze. In 1788, Emperor Qianlong needed to find a way to stop the river's floods, which were killing thousands of people every year and destroying homes and crops. He had nine iron oxen made and lowered them into the middle of the river as an offering to the river guardians. Unfortunately, it didn't work. That year, the floods were even worse than usual.

Swimming the Yangtze

In 1956, AFTER YEARS OF TURMOIL and civil war, a communist government led by Mao Zedong was in power in China. But Mao was worried—some people opposed the Communist Party, and he wasn't able to make the changes he wanted fast enough. He needed to prove that he was a strong and confident leader. What better way to do that than by swimming the country's most powerful river?

One summer day, accompanied by 30 guards, 8 security boats, 4 speedboats, and various friends and government officials, Mao waded out into the fast-flowing water of the Yangtze near the city of Wuhan, about 1,000 kilometers (620 miles) inland from Shanghai. His swim across to the far bank of the river took about two hours. The stunt worked—Mao's swim became famous all across the country, and support for China's courageous leader shot up.

Mao used his popularity to bring in a program he called the Great Leap Forward. It was intended to make China as rich as countries in North America and Europe. But the plan didn't work. In fact, many people became poorer, and thousands starved when the government tried to change farming methods.

Ten years later, at the age of 73, Mao decided it was time to go back to the Yangtze for another demonstration of his power. Swimming along with him this time were 5,000 schoolchildren, factory workers, and supporters. It was a party in the Yangtze, broadcast on the news all over the world. Again Mao used his victory over the river to make big changes in China: he created a movement he called the Cultural Revolution. Like the Great Leap Forward, it caused a lot of suffering to many people, and eventually it had to be abandoned. But Mao wasn't out of ideas yet.

Dam It!

One of the earliest dams we know of was built on the Nile: the Egyptians dammed the river near the ancient city of Memphis in 2900 BCE. The first Chinese dam wasn't built for another 1,700 years—and it was on a tributary of the Yangtze.

The World's Biggest Dam

DAMMING THE YANGTZE had originally been suggested in 1919 by Sun Yat-sen, the country's first president. He argued a dam would help control flooding downstream, provide water to irrigate crops, and generate huge amounts of electricity to power China's growing industries. Forty years later, Mao decided to build the biggest, most powerful dam the world had ever seen, on the Yangtze River.

It took nearly 50 years, but eventually Mao's vision came true: the Three Gorges Dam opened in 2012. It was built even though many scientists and environmentalists in China and around the world opposed the project. They warned that giant dams on the world's other mighty rivers had caused great environmental damage, with terrible consequences for the health of the rivers. Whole villages and towns had to be moved to make way for the enormous lake created behind the Three Gorges Dam, and no one knows what the long-term effects will be.

THE NEWCOMER: SUN YAT-SEN

In 1911, there was a revolution in China, and the emperor was defeated. It was the moment a man named Sun Yat-sen had been waiting for. Sun was a revolutionary who hoped to lead China into the modern age. He was in exile in America at the time but he raced back to China to take the lead of the new government. One of his first acts was to declare the country's new capital: Nanjing. The city was strategically located in China's heartland, the rich Yangtze River Valley.

Sun Yat-sen's government didn't last long. There were years of war and turmoil ahead for China. But Sun Yat-sen remains in the city he loved. His huge mausoleum (the building that holds his tomb) is located there, at the foot of a mountain looking out over Nanjing and the wide brown Yangtze winding through it.

A headwater stream of the Yangtze, known as the Red River

The dam is just one of the challenges the Yangtze faces. It's also becoming polluted from the factories built along its banks and by the chemicals used on crops grown in the Yangtze basin. Dai Qing, a Chinese environmentalist, remembers that the river used to be so clear, if you dropped a pen into the water you could watch it sink all the way to the bottom. Today, the murky water is no longer safe to drink. But environmentalists like Dai are helping to change that. They're restoring wetlands along the Yangtze, encouraging farmers to use organic methods instead of chemicals, and teaching local people about the dangers of pollution—all to ensure a healthy future for the river.

Apache men working on Hoover Dam construction, 1932

THE COLORADO RIVER: WATER TO THE DESERT

Built in 1935, the Hoover Dam is on the lower reaches of the Colorado River, in the U.S. state of Nevada. It is 221 meters (726 feet) high and contains more masonry (concrete or stone for building) than the Great Pyramid of Giza. The Hoover Dam was built during the Great Depression, when many Americans were out of work and desperately poor, and the dam came to symbolize the country's hope for the future. If U.S. citizens could create something so massive, so powerful, surely they could survive the Depression.

Today, tourists still drive out into the desert to marvel at the giant dam that revolutionized what people once considered a wasteland. On Lake Mead, the enormous man-made lake behind the dam, speedboats roar by pulling water-skiers. Cruise boats and houseboats bob on the blue waves. Everyone enjoys the golden sunshine. But don't plan on a leisurely picnic here. You'll need to chew your sandwich fast, because in just a few minutes the bread can dry out. Yes, this is still the desert.

Conclusion

THE CHANGES BROUGHT BY RIVERS AREN'T ALL HISTORY; they're busy shaping the world right now. Since the earth was formed, rivers have worn down high mountains and carried off grains of sand, rock, and soil, depositing this treasure along their floodplains to create fertile river valleys and estuaries. They've changed course, cutting new paths through the land. They've unleashed terrible floods that destroyed everything in their path. They've dried up, turning lush areas into barren deserts. And it's all still happening, all over the world.

Humans have always been fascinated by these world-shapers. We've worshipped rivers, feared them, and built civilizations around them. We've depended on them to provide the water and food we need to live. We've battled against rivers, fought each other for control of them, and used them in war. We sing songs and tell stories about them.

From the earliest beginnings of life, rivers have been the source of changes in our world, some good and some bad. We've got more power now than ever before to alter rivers. Yet for all the tools we have today to understand and transform our environment, the ebbing and flowing of rivers can still flood major cities, or send whole regions into crisis over water shortages.

Today, many people are realizing that how we treat our rivers can have a big impact on our lives. Whether it's pollution, dams, or changing climate, our activities on and around rivers can have far-reaching and long-lasting effects. More and more, people are becoming aware that we need to do more to respect and protect our rivers, to ensure we can rely on them now and in the future.

GLOSSARY OF RIVER TERMS

ANASTOMOSING RIVER: a river that has a meandering pattern with many channels

AQUEDUCT: a man-made channel to conduct water, often on a raised bridge structure

BASIN: (drainage basin) the area of land drained by a river and its tributaries

BED: (riverbed) the ground forming the bottom of a river, often consisting of sand and stones

CANAL: a man-made river channel

CHANNEL: the deepest part of a river, often a passageway for boats

CONFLUENCE: the point where two rivers join

DAM: a barrier built across a river to hold back water

DELTA: a flat, low-lying plain formed at the mouth of a river by deposits of sediment

DOWNSTREAM: the direction a river flows, toward the mouth

ESTUARY: the lower course of a river, where salt water flows in to mix with fresh water

FLOODPLAIN: flat land alongside a river that is periodically flooded when the river overflows its banks. Floodplains are fertile land usually used for growing crops

HEADWATER: the source of a river

IRRIGATION: a method of supplying water to farmland by diverting it from rivers through canals, ditches, or pipes

MOUTH: the ending point of a river; the point where a river enters a larger body of water (e.g., the sea)

RAPIDS: fast-flowing stretches of a river where rocks just under the water's surface create waves

REACHES: sections of a river

SEDIMENT/SILT: solid particles of earth or sand carried by moving water and deposited downstream

SOURCE: the starting point of a river (also called the headwater)

TRIBUTARY: a river or stream flowing into a bigger river

ACKNOWLEDGMENTS

Thanks to friends and family for their many "river story" suggestions, and to the tireless reference staff at the Vancouver Public Library and University of British Columbia who helped me track them down. My gratitude as well to the team at Annick, Barbara Pulling and Paula Ayer for their insightful edits, Natalie Olsen for her design, and to Kim for the illustrations that bring the words so beautifully to life.

PHOTO CREDITS

1 Hassan Janali, U.S. Army Corps of Engineers; 3 used by permission of Lee and Thea Savory; 6, 18, 32, 44, 56, 68, 80, 94, 106, 116, and wave images used throughout © Kim Rosen; background textures used throughout © Tomas Jasinskis, © ixer; maps © Peter Hermes Furian; canoe paddles used throughout © marekuliasz; 8 © Alberto Loyo; 10 © Creativemarc; 11 © Fir4ik; 13 © val lawless; 14 © Alexander Kuguchin; 24 © Matteo Gabrieli; 26 © jsp; 29 © Prometheus72; 34 © milosk50; 37 © pterwort; 40 © julius fekete; 46 © Igor Plotnikov; 48 © Matt Apps; 50 © Scirocco340; 52 © Rob Bouwman; 58, 63, 64 © guentermanaus; 60 © ekkstock; 61 © Antonio Clemens; 65 © kwest; 70 © e2dan; 73 © rachisan alexandra; 74 diamonds © everything possible, cocoa beans © Miguel Garcia Saavedra; 75 © Danielle Robichaud; 76 © Martinez de la Varga; 77 © 2630ben; 82 © Neil Mitchell; 83, 85 © Andy Lidstone; 84 © Morphart Creation; 87 © Neveshkin Nikolay; 88 © Ventura; 90 © Sean Pavone; 96 © Joe Ferrer; 98 © Catwalker; 102 © Lucarelli Temistocle; 103 © A. Laengauer; 108 © Nila Newsom; 110 © Darko Sikman; 112 © Hintau Aliaksei; 113 © ChameleonsEye; 118 © rest; 119 © Venjamin Kraskov; 120 © Yu Lan; 121 © PRILL; 122 © Tropinina Olga: all Shutterstock.com; 9 © User:120, Creative Commons Attribution 2.5 Generic License; 15 uploaded by User:120; 123 © Luo Shaoyang, Creative Commons Attribution 2.0 Generic License; 124 courtesy US National Archives: all downloaded from Wikipedia.org; 12 © National Geographic Image Collection; 20 © Network Photographer; 41 © Mike Goldwater: all Alamy; 22 PGA—Muller, A.—Noah's ark (D size); 27 LC-J717-X102-17; 36 LC-M32- 965; 38 LC-M305- SL17-8931; 39 LC-M32- 865; 101 LC-USZ62-127236/New York World-Telegram and the Sun Newspaper Photograph Collection: all courtesy of the Library of Congress Prints and Photographs Division; 23 Frank Hurley (11=885–1962), Scenes taken near Luxor, 23564929; 53 3792787: both courtesy of the National Library of Australia; 47 Courtesy the private collection of Roy Winkelman / ClipArt ETC

SOURCES

General

Coates, Peter. *A Story of Six Rivers: History, Culture and Ecology.* London: Reaktion Books, 2013.

Middleton, Nick. *Rivers: A Very Short Introduction.* Oxford: Oxford University Press, 2012.

Penn, James R. *Rivers of the World: A Social, Geographical, and Environmental Sourcebook.* Santa Barbara, CA: ABC-CLIO, 2001.

Wohl, Ellen. *A World of Rivers: Environmental Change on Ten of the World's Great Rivers.* Chicago: University of Chicago Press, 2011.

Chapter 1: Awash

Ashton, N., S.G. Lewis, I. De Groote, S.M. Duffy, M. Bates et al. "Hominin Footprints from Early Pleistocene Deposits at Happisburgh, UK." *PLos One* 9, no.2 (2014): e 88329. doi:10.1371/journal/pone.0088329.

Johanson, Donald, and Maitland Edey. *Lucy: The Beginnings of Humankind.* New York: Simon and Schuster, 1981.

Johanson, D. C., and M. Taieb. "Plio-Pleistocene hominid discoveries in Hadar, Ethiopia." *Nature* 260 (March 25, 1976): 293–97. doi:10.1038/260293a0.

Palmer, Douglas. *Origins: Human Evolution Revealed.* London: Mitchell Beazley, 2010.

Picq, Pascal, and Nicole Verrechia. *Lucy and Her Times.* New York: Henry Holt & Co., 1996.

Thimmesh, Catherine. *Lucy Long Ago: Uncovering the Mystery of Where We Came From.* Boston: Houghton Mifflin Harcourt, 2009.

Chapter 2: Tigris and Euphrates

Hodge, Trevor A. *Roman Aqueducts and Water Supply.* London: Gerald Duckworth & Co., 2002.

Pollock, Susan, and Rita P. Wright. *Ancient Mesopotamia.* Cambridge: Cambridge University Press, 1999.

Somervill, Barbara A. *Empires of Ancient Mesopotamia.* New York: Chelsea House, 2010.

Chapter 3: Nile

Albinia, Alice. *Empires of the Indus: The Story of a River.* London: John Murray, 2008.

Barghusen, Joan. *Daily Life in Ancient and Modern Cairo.* Minneapolis, MN: Runestone Press, 2001.

Collins, Robert O. *The Nile.* New Haven, CT: Yale University Press, 2002.

Chapter 4: Rhine

Cioc, Mark. *The Rhine: An Eco-Biography.* Seattle, WA: University of Washington Press, 2002.

UNESCO World Heritage Center. "Upper Middle Rhine Valley." United Nations Educational, Scientific and Cultural Organization (UNESCO). whc.unesco.org/en/list/1066

Chapter 5: Amazon

Davis, Wade. "The Forests of Amazonia," in *Shadows in the Sun: Travels to Landscapes of Spirit and Desire*. Washington, DC: Island Press, 1998.

Government of South Australia State Library. "Aboriginal Australians and the River: Aboriginal Life Along the Murray." SA Memory: South Australia: Past and Present, For the Future (website). samemory.sa.gov.au

Hemming, John. *Tree of Rivers: The Story of the Amazon*. New York: Thames & Hudson, 2008.

Knapp, Sandra. *Alfred Russel Wallace: Footsteps in the Forest*. London: Natural History Museum, 2013.

Chapter 6: Zambezi

Greene, Meg. *Jacques Cartier: Navigating the St. Lawrence River*. New York: Rosen Publishing, 2004.

Johnson, Chuck. "The Tonga, the Kariba Dam, and the Angry God (video)." International Rivers, 2013. internationalrivers.org/resources/the-tonga-the-kariba-dam-and-the-angry-god-video-8184

Ross, Andrew. *David Livingstone: Mission and Empire*. London: Hambledon & London, 2002.

Chapter 7: Thames

Ackroyd, Peter. *Thames: Sacred River*. London: Chatto & Windus, 2007.

Leapman, Michael. *London's River: A History of the Thames*. London: Pavilion Books, 1991.

Museum of London. "Frozen Thames: Frost Fair 1684." museumoflondon.org.uk/london-wall/whats-on/exhibitions-displays/frost-fairs

Weightman, Gavin. *London's Thames*. London: John Murray, 2004.

Chapter 8: Mississippi

Beattie, Andrew. *The Danube: A Cultural History*. Oxford: Oxford University Press, 2010.

Johnson, Robin. *The Mississippi: America's Mighty River*. New York: Crabtree Publishing, 2010.

Kenney, William Howland. *Jazz on the River*. Chicago: University of Chicago Press, 2005.

Mour, Stanley I. *American Jazz Musicians*. Springfield, NJ: Enslow Publishers, 1998.

Nott, G. William. "Blanche Leathers, steamboat captain of the Packett Natchez." *Item Tribune*, New Orleans, LA, February 13, 1927.

Chapter 9: Ganges

Singh, Raghubir. *The Ganges*. London: Thames & Hudson, 1992.

Spilsbury, Richard. *Settlements of the Ganges River*. Chicago: Heinemann Library, 2005.

Chapter 10: Yangtze

Davis, Wade. *River Notes: A Natural and Human History of the Colorado*. Washington, DC: Island Press, 2013.

Winchester, Simon. *The River at the Center of the World: A Journey Up the Yangtze and Back in Chinese Time*. New York: Henry Holt & Co., 1996.

Wong, C.M., C.E. Williams, J. Pittock, U. Collier, and P. Schelle. *World's Top 10 Rivers at Risk*. Gland, Switzerland: WWF International, 2007.

INDEX

ABOUT THE AUTHOR

Marilee Peters lives in Vancouver, along a street that was once a salmon stream. If you pause near the sewer grate on a quiet afternoon, you can hear the little river rushing by in the darkness, far below. Listening to that stream, paved over many years ago, made her think about all the ways that rivers affect our lives—sometimes in ways we're not even aware of!

She's also taken a boat ride down the Yangtze River, not far from where the giant Three Gorges Dam is now, and cruised along the Thames through the busy heart of London. Those memories came in handy while writing this book, but what she enjoyed most about writing *10 Rivers That Shaped the World* was learning how throughout history people have been adapting their lives to the rivers that surround them.

Marilee's first book, *Patient Zero: Solving the Mysteries of Deadly Epidemics,* was published in 2014.

ABOUT THE ILLUSTRATOR

Kim Rosen was raised in a suburb of Philadelphia, Pennsylvania, and could usually be found in her room quietly drawing pictures. After high school, Kim studied advertising design at the Fashion Institute of Technology in New York City. She worked as a designer for several years, then realized she was meant to be an illustrator, and moved to Georgia to attend the Savannah College of Art and Design, where she earned an MFA in illustration.

Today Kim lives with her partner in Northampton, Massachusetts, where she can usually be found in her studio quietly drawing pictures for clients all over the world. She has illustrated for magazines (*The New Yorker, The Atlantic*), newspapers (*The Boston Globe, The Globe and Mail*) and corporate clients (Billabong, Starbucks, American Express). For Annick Press, she previously illustrated *10 Plants That Shook the World* by Gillian Richardson and contributed artwork to Shane Koyczan's *To This Day: For the Bullied and Beautiful.*